I, THE SALT DOLL

(*Mee Mithaachi Baahuli*)

I, THE SALT DOLL

(*Mee Mithaachi Baahuli*)

VANDANA MISHRA

Translated from the Marathi by
JERRY PINTO

SPEAKING
TIGER

SPEAKING TIGER PUBLISHING PVT. LTD
4381/4, Ansari Road, Daryaganj
New Delhi 110002

Published originally in Marathi by Rajhans Prakashan, Pune
This English translation first published by
Speaking Tiger in paperback 2016

ISBN: 978-93-85755-76-7
eISBN: 978-93-85755-77-4

10 9 8 7 6 5 4 3 2 1

Typeset in Minion Pro by SÜRYA, New Delhi
Printed at Gopsons Papers Ltd, Noida

This book is for:
My mother Laxmibai Lotlikar
My mother-in-law Kesharbai Mishra
My husband Pandit Jaydeo Mishra
My daughter Kuntala Mishra
Death may have snatched them from me.
But they breathe in my veins.

Many Indian languages and local cultures have their own version of the salt doll story and it is widely believed that the parable sums up the ephemeral nature of life and the vastness of Time. The story goes something like this: A salt doll spends time frolicking on the shore, building sand castles or collecting shells. Enamoured as she is of the deep, calm sea which surrounds her, one day the salt doll decides to enter the blue waters for a good bath. And never returns.

ORIGINALLY, WE'RE FROM GOA. OUR VILLAGE IS LOTLI, which makes us Lotlikars. Our surname is Keni. Keni-Lotlikar would be the correct name but somewhere along the way Keni fell away and Lotlikar remained.

We're Saraswats. Our household deity is Ramnath Kamaksha. The Portuguese committed many atrocities in Goa. They converted thousands by force. Many abandoned their homes, taking their Gods with them. The entire community was scattered and Goan society disrupted.

Our forefathers took refuge in the Konkan, in the Rajapur district of Ratnagiri. There have been Lotlikars there for two hundred years now. There were many changes in the way we lived because of this shift. Konkani faded away and we began to speak a local dialect of Marathi. '*Toos kaay paahijé*?' (What do you want?) one of us might ask while Saraswat Punekari Marathi would have it as, '*Tula kaay paahijé*? We began to eat as the Konkanis do too, less fish for a start. Our staple diet became rice with buttermilk and vegetables; or ricewater and vegetables. We ate fish but didn't make too much of a song and dance about it. The fisherwoman would come to the back of the house, and we would ritually purify the fish by sprinkling water over and around it. We were lucky that our tradition did not require us to wash the fish with soap. Our diction and pronunciations were clear but our voices rather high-pitched. We spoke loudly, nasally, as if we were scolding each other.

*

My mother, who I called Aai, was Lakshmibai Lotlikar. She was a Goan, a Karmarkar. She was originally called Putalabai. The Lotlikars changed this to Lakshmibai when she married into their family. My father's name was Narayan Govind Lotlikar. So Mother was Lakshmibai Narayan Lotlikar.

My mother was fifteen when she got married. After their marriage, my parents came to Mumbai. My father was an accountant in the Bhuleshwar office of Anant Shivaji Desai. Topiwale Desai, as he was known, was the owner of one of the most famous firms of the time. My parents settled down in Mandodari Chawl in the Lamington Road area. This was in 1918. Two years later, Lokmanya Tilak would pass away at Sardargriha, the famous hotel in south Mumbai. His funeral drew an enormous procession of mourners, Aai would say.

We were three siblings. Kashi was the eldest, born in 1922. Next came Prahlad (Babu as he was called) in 1924 and me in 1927 on January 26. Later, the country would become independent and January 26 would be the day on which the Constitution came into force and it became our Republic Day, a day to be celebrated across the country. And so my birthday became a matter of national importance.

My father died suddenly when I was about two or

thereabouts. Aai says it was double pneumonia that took him. It all happened very quickly. His friends and colleagues did their best but before we knew it, he was gone. The office staff took over all the funeral arrangements. Aai was only twenty-three or twenty-four then but death was no stranger to her: the plague had decimated her family. However, the sudden demise of her husband shook the foundations of her world.

I do not remember a single thing about my father. He must have loved me deeply; he probably spoiled me and brought me sweets to eat. I remember nothing of this. I didn't even see him in a photograph. In those days, photographs were not commonplace. Only wealthy families were in the habit of going to studios to have photographs taken.

He was a tall man, I am told. He was strong and stout, well-built, with a dusky complexion, a smile always on his face. He wore a dhotar that reached his ankles, a shirt, a coat and a topi. With such slim pickings, I have had to conjure up the image of my father. The image is vague, tentative, but I fold my hands in front of it and offer the salutation of a namaskaar.

*

After he died, Aai decided to go and live in the Konkan. Our family was from Adivré and she was prepared to spend the rest of her life there. All said and done, Mumbai was a strange city for us. We had no close relations to hand. Aai felt she would not be able to bring up three young children there. At least the Lotlikars had an ancestral home in Adivré. There were also some fields. In the Mandodari

Chawl, we had a neighbour called Nadkarni. He was my father's colleague. He too advised my mother to return home. 'Mumbai is a huge city. You won't be able to get by here. And the children are so young.' Mrs Nadkarni agreed. They even gave us our fare home. All I recall of that journey is the rolling of the ship and the wide expanses of the sea.

We spent only ten or twelve days at our commonly-held ancestral home in Adivré. My father's maternal uncle, Sakharam Appa, lived there. He made it clear to us, in word and deed, that we were not wanted. Sakharam Appa made a savage condition for us to stay: 'You will have to shave your head if you want to stay here,' he told Aai. Aai's stomach went hollow at these words. Widows were treated badly in those days. There was always a mountain of work for them to do. They had to keep their heads bowed. They could not be seen laughing or talking; in fact, it was felt that they should not be seen much at all. They were not allowed food with spices in it. They were given only leftovers. They had to bear the slights and taunts of everyone in the family. Aai announced that she was not going to be shaved. Appa didn't like that one bit.

The other issue was our education. Aai wanted all of us to study up to the matriculation level at least. Sakharam Appa thought otherwise. 'What's the point of educating girls? They're supposed to help with the housework. Isn't there enough for them to do at home? They'll learn what they need to know.' He put a huge broom into Prahlad's hands. 'Go and clear the fields,' he said. Aai got the point.

We had to live according to Appa's rules. His was the

last word in that house. He kept everyone in a state of fear. He was a large man with a stern face. His day would begin with two measures of kanji and a liberal helping of buttermilk and one onion. Then he would go out. He walked with so heavy a tread one could almost feel the ground trembling under his feet. His slippers would scrip-scrape scrip-scrape as he walked. We were very scared of him.

Aai decided to return to Mumbai. When we left Adivré, we made our namaskaars to everyone, including Sakharam Appa.

'We have a share in this house,' Aai said. (Or something like that.)

Sakharam Appa was enraged. 'Don't talk about your share. Your ornaments should be enough.'

That he gave us our return fares was a stroke of good luck. 'Take your fares and go,' he said.

Once more, the ship. Once again, the sea, the sea. Water, water everywhere and in Aai's eyes too.

*

Aai had decided to place her faith in the city. We returned to Mandodari Chawl. It was Diwali and every house had oil lamps welcoming Lakshmi, goddess of wealth; every home was filled with the rich aromas of festival food cooking. Only our home was dark. The fireflies must have looked to Lakshmibai like question marks dancing in the darkness: How shall I live? How shall I bring up my children?

There was also the loan from the Nadkarnis, our neighbours. How was that to be repaid? 'Let me wash your clothes for you. You don't have to pay me until I've worked off the loan,' Aai told Mrs Nadkarni, almost as soon as we returned. Poor Nadkarni Vahini[1] was fit to weep. She refused but Aai would not give up. She would not live on charity. She believed that if you couldn't pay in cash, you could always pay with work. It was a principle she would live by.

On the second day of Diwali, Nadkarni Vahini brought a bucket of clothes and left it in front of our door, early in the morning. And in a quiet voice, she told my sister, 'Kaashé, tell your Mum not to dump the clothes out all at once. I've put something in the bottom.'

That 'something' was a container with sweets in it. Our father had just died. If Nadkarni Vahini had brought the container of festival sweets and savouries to us during the day, people would have commented: 'Their father's ashes haven't cooled and they're gobbling laddoos and karanjis.' That was why Nadkarni Vahini had concealed the sweets among the clothes and left them there in the quiet of the morning.

'Will you spend your life washing clothes?' she asked Aai. 'Think about the future too.' Aai got the point. One day, she took all three children and plonked herself down at Shivaji Topiwale's office.

'Arré, it's Narayan's wife,' said Mr Desai and rose to his feet. Aai gave him the short version of what had happened in Adivré.

Mr Desai was touched by our plight. 'Vahini, do not

[1]By calling Mrs Nadkarni 'Vahini' or sister-in-law, the author makes Mr Nadkarni into a brother and thus emphasizes the closeness of their relationship or their love for her.

be afraid. We'll figure something out. Don't lose courage,' he said. He told his manager to arrange accommodation for us in Lakshmi Chawl in Lamington Road, an area full of chawls. If we had continued at Mandodari, we would have had to pay rent and where was the money to come from? Lakshmi Chawl belonged to Anant Shivaji Desai. The manager brought us some cooking pots, a stove and basic supplies for a couple of months. He would come regularly over the next few months and top them up. But within a year, Aai was working.

*

Lakshmi Chawl was a mud building of four storeys. There were about thirty-five tenants. Many of these were Gaud Saraswats; some were Kudaldeshkars. All the rooms were big and had two beams. We had a single room. The toilet and water tap were outside. Each home had a *mori*, a tiled area for washing. There was lots of water but electricity had not reached the rooms yet. In the nights, we lit oil lamps. They were high-maintenance things. One had to clean off the lampblack, fill them with oil, trim the wick. This was generally the children's work. There was a light bulb in the chawl but it was turned on late at night. Bhaiyya was in charge of this. *Bhaiyya* literally means brother. Later another meaning would attach itself to the word: that of a man from North India, from Bihar or Uttar Pradesh. In the old system in Mumbai, our bhaiyyas had their place but political forces suddenly made them outsiders. 'Bhaiyya' was in charge of collecting the rent and making sure the water was flowing and the light bulb was working.

Lakshmi Chawl was right in front of Lamington Road

Police Station. Every morning there would be a police parade. All the children would crowd the verandah to watch. The British sergeant looked very smart. The sepoys went in fear of him. At the morning turn-out he would run an eagle eye over their uniforms, footwear, putties and copper buttons. If the uniform were not shipshape, if the buttons did not shine, he would ring a peal over their heads. The sepoys would be terrified and so would we, the children of the chawl. If one of the constables was a bit worse for the wear, he would get a resounding thump on the back. This meant that the police were always in good shape. In our youth, we saw no ungainly paunches, no scrawny bodies among the law-keepers. Nor were there men who would extort bribes from the vegetable vendors, the tradesmen or the shopkeepers. If there were one or two, they conducted themselves with discretion. We called policemen, 'Dada', elder brother. Like 'Bhaiyya' this word, too, was part of an old city.

*

We settled down nicely in Lakshmi Chawl. Mr Desai came to visit. He stood outside our room and asked after us. When he left, he asked our neighbour, Mr Wagle to 'keep an eye on them'. Wagle had two children, a boy and a girl. The girl was called 'Babi' at home. My mother also called me 'Babi' and Prahlad was 'Babu'. Kashi was only called Kashi and she was very proud of that. When you said her name, you were invoking a holy place, Aai would say.

Kashi and Prahlad were names with religious resonance. When I was born, my father told Aai, 'Let's name her in a more modern tradition.' And so I was named

Sushila. It was only later that names beginning with the prefix 'Su' (or good) became fashionable and multiplied.

One day, a man came from Anant Shivaji Desai's office. He told Aai, 'You have been put in for training at J J Hospital[2].' Mr Desai had told our story to Dr Karande and Dr Bhangle, both well-known doctors of the time. Their word was law. At that time too, widowed, orphaned and abandoned women were seen as suitable candidates for the nursing or teaching professions. Aai's formal education had ended after the second standard. It would have taken a long time and much money to train her as a teacher. The course in midwifery was, on the other hand, easy and short. In a year, Aai had learned the ropes and was ready to work. The good doctors got her a job at the J J Hospital. We found it quite funny that Aai was going to school just as we were.

At that time, Shrirang Mama came to stay with us. He was Aai's paternal cousin. He had studied up to the matriculation. He had exquisite handwriting. He had come to Mumbai to look for a job.

'You stay here for a few months, now,' Aai told him. 'I have to go for training. You can keep an eye on the kids.' He agreed. Aai would cook the rice and dal or amti in the morning and leave for her classes. On some lucky Sundays, she might cook fish. Wagle Kaku from next door would also pop across to keep an eye on us. But it fell to Shrirang Mama to take us kids 'to the tap', our way of saying that he

---

[2]The Sir Jamshetjee Jeejeebhoy Hospital, Byculla, was one of the largest public hospitals in India. It began in 1845 as a School of Practice, where the young doctors studying at the Grant Medical College, could learn their trade.

would have to take us to the toilet. Laxmi Chawl's public 'taps' had a flock of pigeons in residence. They were always in a grey flap about something. For some reason, I was terrified of them. I would wonder when Aai would finally come home. And then one day, the nine-month course was over. The days had flown, like pigeons.

*

We began to go to the Lamington Road Municipality Boys and Girls School. It was a stone building, three storeys of it, a tough-looking thing. The fourth 'floor' was a terrace where we would perform drill. We had no school uniforms. We wore the clothes we wore at home to school but you couldn't tell the rich kids from the poor ones. Up to the second or third standard, the girls wore frocks. In the fifth, we would shift to parkar-polka, a blouse and long skirt. The boys wore shorts and shirts. All the children were from ordinary homes. Why would rich kids be sent to a municipality school?

In reality, we did not see too many rich people then. They lived at Hughes Road, Malabar Hill, those areas. Their children went to English-medium schools.

There were thirty to thirty-five girls in each class. (The boys sat in a different class.) We sat at benches that could be folded up. Once the teacher said, 'Fold your benches,' you hopped up and folded your bench. School began at eleven a.m. and ended at five. It was like a full-time job. Our lunch break was from one to two. All three of us would come home to eat dal and rice. And then we would go back to school. Sometimes Aai would give us one or two paise. Then we would buy sev and sweet boondis, chikki or something like that. Otherwise it would be guavas or berries or sugarcane sticks. Our school-teacher would often say, 'Eat chikki, it's good for health. Chikki has groundnut and jaggery.' Whether this is indeed healthy or not, I don't know. Once, I dragged Aai to a restaurant near school and ordered myself a glass of piyush, a drink of buttermilk and shrikhand. It cost three paise. For two paise you could get a bellyful of sev-boondi. That was our idea of fun.

Shantabai Kashalkar[3] was our principal. She sat at the main school in Gowalia Tank. Once a fortnight, she would make a trip to our school. From the first to the fourth standard, I had Varutai Padhye as my class-teacher. In the fifth standard, Bodhebai arrived. Our art teacher was Brahmandkarbai. Hirabai Jhaveri[4] taught us music. At that time, she was quite well-known. Shyamalabai Mazgaonkar and she were sisters. They ran a music class near Central Cinema. Later, Sita and Madhubala, Hirabai's daughters, also became quite famous in the world of music.

All the teachers wore nine-yard saris and blouses. They wore their nine-yard saris differently from the Saraswats. Few wore any jewellery. If they did, it would be limited to small studs in the ears and two or three bangles. They were all quite simply dressed. Brahmandkarbai would wear a stole too. On her feet she would have red Brahmin slippers.

Varutai Padhye was our class teacher. When she came

---

[3]Very little seems to be known about Mrs Shantabai Kashalkar but we know from *Film India* that she rose to be Municipal Inspector of Schools and that she was also associated with the Bombay Presidency Social Reform Association which worked on many issues including child marriage and temperance.
[4]Marathi bhavgeet singer of some repute.

into the class all the children had to rise to their feet and say, '*Namaste, bai*.' Then she would take attendance. One or two girls might be absent. If anyone was absent for three or four days at a stretch, the teacher would send the school sepoy to the house to inquire about her health. Or she might ask the girl's friends. Our world was a small cosy one.

The girls generally behaved well and looked out for each other. We all knew each other's homes. Most of us came from the same sort of home. You could tell the richer girls by the leather bags they carried. All the rest of us carried plain cloth bags.

The teachers in the girls' section never carried canes. I was never beaten in all my years at school. That honour was reserved for the boys. For us girls, the thought that the teacher might get angry and scold us was enough to keep us in line. But we knew that the scolding came from a loving place. In those days there was no such thing as sex education. But when we got to the sixth or seventh standard, the teacher would talk in a roundabout fashion about menstruation. 'If something strange happens to you, don't worry about it. Come and tell me,' she might say. Then some girls would start their periods. By the time a girl was fourteen or fifteen, she would move from parkar-polka and would be swaddled in saris forever after.

My first parkar-polka was made of Dharwadi *khunn* with a broad border. At the age of thirteen, I made the shift to saris. Aai got me one for two rupees. It was pink with a green border.

The classrooms were large with big windows that allowed the light in and let breezes blow all day long.

There was much emphasis on learning by heart. In the last hour of school, we were supposed to recite together all the poems, Sanskrit shlokas, tables and whatever else we had learned during the day. In the fourth standard we learned Reverend N V Tilak's *Kshanokshani Pade* (Falling All the Time). Our teacher recited it through a veil of tears. The girls were crying too. I thought of my mother and I missed her and cried all the harder. The teacher tried to console me. It was a heart-warming sight.

The *Navayug Vachanmala* (The New Era Reader), edited by Acharya Atre, had some rather good prose and poetry. We were all at a formative age. When we read something good, it seemed to pervade our minds, as if light were gradually dispelling the darkness. And yet, an inexplicable melancholy would fill the heart. In that state we would come home. In comparison to the children of today, we were not very street-smart. But we did develop an ability to appreciate beauty, to find it and hold on to it and to face what was ugly in life as well. That is what I think a real education should do for you.

We were also taught the Modi script[5] in school. We learned how to calculate pounds, shillings and pence. We learned the multiplication tables from two onwards, taking in the two-and-a-half times tables and doing vertical tables as well. Recitation made our pronunciation clear and our memory sharp.

Our school celebrated Dassehra in great style. We were expected to draw a pattern representing Saraswati on

[5]The Modi script was used for Marathi until the twentieth century.

our slates, using only the numeral one and bring flowers and coconuts to school in the morning. Then the teacher would arrange all of them beautifully. There would be a collective pooja. Every girl would get jaggery, channa and coconut as prasad. We would have to recite the prayer, '*Ya Kundendu tushaar haar dhavala*' (Salutations to She who is white as jasmine, cool as the moon and shines like a string of pearls), all together, of course. Saraswati would be seated in padmasana in the middle, dressed in white, bedecked with white flowers and garlands.

In truth, the children in the Lamington Road School did not have much to do with the British Raj. The sun might never set on the British Empire but it didn't shine on us much. Even so, on the King's birthday, we would be given some sweets. I suspect it was like a bribe so that we might feel some sympathy for His Majesty. Our love was to be bought from us, it seems. Once they even distributed some nickel coins as well. We should not have fallen prey to all these temptations. Truly, I regret eating those sweets with such joy.

One day, Hirabai Jhaveri suggested that I join her music class near Central Cinema. I said, 'I'll ask my mother.' So Aai went to see the class. She made thorough inquiries about Hirabai and who else studied there and what went on.

'Lakshmibai, you should not worry at all. I myself teach the girls to sing. I also take care of all the administration,' said Hirabai. I began to go to class three times a week, right after school. There were about eight or ten girls who studied under her. Hirabai herself played the harmonium and accompanied us. The first raga I studied with her was *Bhoop*, an exceptionally sweet and melodious raga. I enjoyed the class immensely. I must have had a good voice and the ability to stay in tune and keep the rhythm. Perhaps that is why Hirabai did not take any fees from me. 'You have a lovely voice, Babi. Work hard and practise as much as you can. You will become famous in the future,' Hirabai said to me.

The Shri Swami Samarth School thus introduced me to an infinity of music. As soon as the harmonium began to play I would lose myself, my mind slipping into butterfly mode, fluttering over the music. Hirabai was a fine teacher. She would explain the *chalan*, the catchphrase of the raag, its ascending and descending patterns beautifully. She taught us two songs—*Niki niki taan chatur sunaai* (Sing with simplicity, clarity and intelligence) and *Naa maanoongi, naa maanoongi, naa maanoongi, main toh unhi ke manaaye bina* (I will listen to no one and nothing until he explains himself to me). They were rhythmic and had lovely tunes and we liked them very much.

That well-educated girls from good Marathi families were now learning music seemed like a big thing to me. But then Maharashtra was the scene of many social movements. Mahatma Phule, Justice Mahadev Govind Ranade, Pandita Ramabai, Tarabai Shinde, Maharishi Dhondo Keshav Karve had all contributed to the reform of Maharashtrian society. They had shown the way for the education of all classes and castes, for the education of women too. Women were already making great strides in education. That meant that new winds were blowing through our society. This could also be the reason why our mother had refused to let her hair be chopped off in

Adivré and had returned to Mumbai to train as a nurse and how I, in turn, had begun to learn music.

The other reason was that Maharashtra was an important centre for classical music. Pandit Vishnu Digambar Paluskar and Pandit Vishnu Narayan Bhatkhande had spread education about classical music in the pre-Independence period. Several music classes had been begun in different places across the country, all the way to Karachi. The Gwalior, Agra, Jaipur-Atrauli and Kirana gharanas were also popular among the people and then there was Marathi theatre, All India Radio and the gramophone companies all doing their bit to bring music into every home. Saraswati had planted the seeds of music in Maharashtra's fertile soil and rich were the fruits of the crop. I was a blade of grass in that orchard.

At the end of Aai's training period at J J Hospital, she received a certificate and was appointed as a midwife in Dr Tilak's Maternity Home at a monthly salary of forty rupees. Aai was delighted and so were we. 'I was lucky to have got this training,' she would say.

Dr Haribhau Tilak was then a well-known gynaecologist. He had entered into partnership with Dr Kaikini and together they had opened the Tilak-Kaikini Hospital at Opera House. The hospital took up an entire floor of the famous Mantri Building. It was spick and span. It had fifteen beds, an operation theatre and if you went a little further, a kitchen. When Aai was on night duty, she would eat in the hospital. It was simple food, vegetarian but tasty.

If she were on day shift, Aai would cook and leave the house at around eleven or eleven-thirty and return at around nine p.m. Night duty meant she had to reach around six or six-thirty and would return at around eight a.m. When she had night duty, Aai would lock us into the house. Our neighbour Sonpatki and his wife would keep an eye on us. We called Mrs Sonpatki, Nanda's Aai. Nanda was her elder son. He was actually Nandkishore, shortened to Nanda. If we wanted anything, we would knock on the window and she would open the door. Generally, wanting something meant wanting to go to the toilet but fortunately such moments did not happen very often. You went once in the morning and you didn't want to go there again all day. You couldn't say you wanted to go 'there' again and again.

Our code word for the toilet was 'The tap at the back'. If you said you were going to the tap at the back, everyone in the chawl understood where you were going. 'The tap in the front' was the clean water tap where we went to fill drinking water and the water with which to wash our clothes and vessels. Most of the young men in the chawl also bathed at the tap in the front. The tap at the back had only one job to do but it was the big job. No one knew who started the tradition of using these names. But each chawl had its own terminology and so a vocabulary specific to Laxmi Chawl came into being. Only we knew what it meant.

When Aai joined the Tilak-Kaikini hospital, we left Laxmi Chawl and moved to Prabhu Nivas. Aai said to Desai's manager, 'I have a job. Now I can afford a room of my own. You must give this room in Laxmi Chawl to someone in need.' And so we moved to Prabhu Nivas. It was a nice big place but it had a water problem. And so we moved again, to Ramji Purushottam Chawl and there we stayed.

In those days, getting a house was very easy. All you had to do was tie up your belongings, take the children by the hand and move. There was no problem of deposit or 'pagdi'. You could change within a chawl, at will. You just had to tell the bhaiyya, 'Bhaiyya, we don't want that first floor room; we are moving to the corner of the second floor.' The bhaiyya would say, 'Go on then' and we would pack up our things and move to the new space.

*

This was 1935 to 1937. During the time of the Second World War, things changed dramatically in Mumbai. Before that, most of the houses stood empty. Most of the chawls were owned by Gujarati Bhatias or Muslims. Islam does not allow the charging or taking of interest and people say that it is for this reason that the Khojas and Memons built chawls in those days. It was a form of investment. Where we lived in Girgaon (or Girgaum as it is also known), there were also a few chawls that rich Marathi men had built.

The owner of the Ramji Purushottam Chawl was a Gujarati. We never set eyes on him. But then all the chawl owners were absentee landlords, swathed in an air of mystery. They might be mystery men but we didn't let them bother us much. If you paid your rent on the nail, you didn't have to worry much about cosying up to your landlord. Mumbaikars were aware of their civic rights and freedoms.

If a family found itself in distress, if the earning member were to lose his job or some dread disease were to manifest, the owner might well waive the rent or allow some credit. These were the only indications of their presence. Otherwise, their agents were the bhaiyyas, who conducted the affairs of the Ram Rajya of the chawls.

Ramji Purushottam Chawl's bhaiyya was Samrath. He was a North Indian. He lived in a single room in the chawl, about the breadth of a man's handspan, with two or three other men, all squish-squashed in. Every three or four months, new men would arrive. Samrath seemed to have voluntarily taken on the responsibility of finding them jobs. His family was a far-flung tribe that reached all the way into the distant suburbs of Ghatkopar, Bhandup, Jogeshwari and Malad.

He might have been pushing sixty but he wandered the chawl like a leopard on the prowl. He would gather news and views even as he kept up a steady rubbing of the tobacco he had cupped in one palm. He was the custodian of the chawl's culture. People did not mind him much but they didn't cross him either. He was an affectionate old fellow for all that. Even if you missed three or four months' rent, he wouldn't complain much. From time to time, he'd remind my mother, 'Lachhmi, it's time to pay the rent.' He spoke to everyone in this informal manner.

If a school-going boy were seen at the corner paan-and-cigarette shop, he would warn the boy's parents. 'Take the boy in hand,' he'd say, but his concern and affection would be evident. If the boy were to plead a case of mistaken identity—'It wasn't me *a-tall*'—his parents would come back with: 'So Samrath's telling lies now?'

Smoking and drinking were considered vices and the parents of the chawl were not dead-set on excusing their children's bad habits as they seem to be doing today.

The residents of the chawl had Samrath's support in this respect.

Every morning, at the crack of dawn, he would be at the tap, bathing and singing bhajans to Maruti or Hanuman. He would check that the water was flowing in 'the tap at the front'. After he had kneaded the dough for his chapattis and prepared the veggie of the day, he would set out to uncover the happenings in the chawl. He would wear a dhotar and his chest would either be bare or covered with a short shirt. The keys would be tied to his sacred thread. He would be humming, '*Maarat kilkaari chale Hanuman*,' (Burbling happily, Little Hanuman trots along) as he went on his rounds. He would have fit perfectly into a Hrishikesh Mukherjee film, would Samrath.

All of Ramji Purushottam Chawl was divided into three chawls: the front, the back and the middle. The front and the back sections were joined by two narrow passages. Each floor had a common passage. On one side of this passage, the rooms stood in a row. On the other side was the parapet. If you stood at the rail at the front of the chawl, you could see the street, the people, the cars, the shops, and if you craned your neck, a fraction of the sky. The back also had a ledge but there was nothing to see so the small fry gathered in the front.

We lived in the middle in Kholi Number 49, first floor. We had two rooms between us. The kitchen had a *mori*, a tiled washing area, and a window. The other room was just a little bigger. Above the door was a transom. That was our ventilation. The first room had no window at all. Light was in short supply in the house. This was because the wall of the front of the chawl was right in front of us, as if a hefty Pathan were in the door, demanding the interest on a loan. There were about seventy families in Ramji Purushottam Chawl, almost all of them Marathi. Perhaps one or two Gujaratis. The chawl was mudwork, all of it, but well-built and robust. It still stands on the corner of Prarthana Samaj. In our time, we paid eighteen rupees rent. It must be a bit more now.

*

Slowly, we settled in. Aai remained at the Tilak-Kaikini Hospital for about a year or a year and a half. She became an expert at all the aspects of childbirth. She even assisted Dr Tilak in the operating theatre. She knew the names of all the instruments by heart. She even began answering the telephone. She could not understand why one had to say 'Hello' when one answered the phone. Why didn't people just start speaking, she wanted to know. Such an important question must not have occurred even to those who invented telephony. Did the telephone come first or the hello? Were people not to say hello, they might come to the point immediately. Much time might be saved. So these speculations might have some worth then?

From time to time, a gynaecologist called Dr Saibai Ranade would visit Dr Haribhau Tilak's hospital. She had a maternity home on Princess Street. She paid special attention to Aai's work. 'My hospital has only just begun,' she told Dr Tilak three or four times, 'I need good people. Please tell Lakshmibai to work for me.' After a period of indecision, Aai did go to work at Dr Ranade's nursing home. She received a magnificent raise of twenty rupees a month, making her salary sixty rupees. Aai was pleased and so were we. Her daily routine did not change. She would travel to Princess Street from Prarthana Samaj by tram. The ticket cost one anna. You could ride right up to Colaba on that much. Four seats on the tram were reserved for women.

Short and stout, Dr Saibai was my ideal in those days. She had been widowed in childhood but she was intelligent and courageous. She had studied medicine in Pune and then opened her maternity home in Mumbai. She wore only pastel colours: yellow, blue or pink five-yard saris. She spoke excellent English, looked smart and had a mild nature.

Saibai's maternity home was small, with only ten beds. It was generally Gujarati ladies who came there and so the door of the clinic had a plate that said, '*Suvavad khatoon*' (Maternity Ward) in Gujarati. Aai helped Dr Ranade with almost every aspect of nursing but the doctor relied heavily on her in Caesarean section cases.

At the time, it didn't seem to matter to the parents if they had a boy or a girl. When the first child was a girl, the mother and those who came to see her, would exclaim, '*Pehli beti ane dhanani peti*' (A girl first? Behold!/She's a pot of gold) with glee. Aai maintained that the parents made no distinction between boys and girls. They took the baby home with faces wreathed in smiles. And by Gujarati tradition, all the staff at the hospital would be given tips. This meant at least another thirty rupees a month added to Aai's kitty. Sometimes boxes of sweets as well. We wished for lots of babies to be born. Perhaps our wishes did come true. Look at the city's population today.

Meanwhile, the three of us were doing well in school.

Aai's job meant stability in our lives. We could even afford a few luxuries, small ones, but we made the most of them. I did well at school; I was good at studies. I had a special liking for History and Marathi but Mathematics was my weakness. My elder sister Kashi was excellent, academically speaking. Mathematics was child's play to her. Hardly had the teacher posed the problem and Kashi had the answer. She was also good at crochet, embroidery and making crepe paper flowers. Her rangolis were exquisite, if temporary, works of art. I loved drawing these patterns in rice flour too. One Diwali, both of us collaborated on a tortoise with two heads. It had fifty points on each side. It took three hours. We were really sweating over it. Even the two-headed tortoise must have thought, 'These girls are really taking their own sweet time.'

Prahlad was doing well too. It was true that he liked to bunk school now and then. But his English was good. After the seventh standard, he joined the Orient High School at Girgaon. In the eighth standard, he chose French as an optional subject. Later, he would solve the *Times of India* crossword in twenty minutes. But I'm getting ahead of myself.

One day, Prahlad got a rather severe beating from Aai. He was still in the Lamington Road High School, in the fifth or sixth standard. Who knows what came over him but he played truant and spent the day loitering in a nearby garden. When he did this again and again, over three days, the class teacher sent a message home. The next day Aai made enquiries and went to the garden. There was Babu on the swings. With a whack here and a thwack there, Aai dragged him to school and handed him over to the master. That evening, Babu did come home but he was a timid creature, terrified of repercussions, his stomach home to a million butterflies. When Aai returned from the hospital, she explained things to him in a gentle way. 'You have no father to shelter you from the winds of chance. If you don't study, we have no future. And neither will you. You must study as much as you can, as hard as you can and only then will you get a good job.' After that Babu never gave her a day's trouble.

As the head of the house, all responsibility fell on Aai's shoulders. She did not even have the time to mourn her husband's untimely death. She focussed on the present, on how to overcome what confronted her, on how to find a way through. She sealed off her own grief and turned her attention on us. The effect of all this was that she became tough; the much-vaunted softness of femininity faded. Her voice acquired an authoritative ring. She was also always alert. 'You can never let your guard down,' she would say. 'From the threshold of your home outwards, you must be aware that you are in a strange and unknown place,' she would insist. We didn't pay her much heed. To us Mumbai was like a good and familiar friend. You could wander at will through the lanes and bylanes. Today, seventy-five years later, I tell people what Aai used to tell us. You can no longer treat the world as your oyster. You have to be aware, to beware in fact. But how is one to form any relationships at all, if one is constantly manning one's borders? What a terrible dichotomy Mumbai has come to represent.

We were lucky in our neighbours. On our left was Nanda's Mum, on the right, the Chaudhuris. Nanda's Dad went off to work; they got the *Lokmanya* newspaper at home. Nanda had a younger brother, Suresh. Everyone called him Bhaavdya. Many years later, Nanda's mother found herself in an interesting condition again. She was delighted to bear a daughter. If Kashi or I were going out, Bhaavdya would whine: 'Take me wif you, no, please?' He would brook no refusals. 'Please, please, take me ouf,' he would shout and plunk himself down.

We would have to take him with us. It did not matter whether we were going to the temple or to the grocer's; Bhaavdya was happy to come. And such was his joy that we ended up swinging him along by his arms all the way to our destination. Later Bhaawdya would swing right up—he became a lawyer.

The Sonpatkis were a Pune family. Their Ganpati puja lasted for one-and-a-half days and it seemed as if all of Sadashiv Peth would arrive for the celebrations. The men would sleep in the balcony wherever they could find place and the women slept inside. At dawn, Nanda's Mum's routine began. The men would bathe at the front tap, mumbling the names of the rivers as a shloka to bless and purify the water. The aarti would be sung with gusto. The whole chawl would be redolent with the smell of camphor, incense and oil lamps. We would get jaggery and coconut, laddoos, sev-chivda and steamed modaks to eat. When the statue of Ganpati was borne away to be ritually immersed, Nanda's Mum would draw her sari pallu over her eyes and weep.

She was a stout woman with a round face and a wheatish complexion. She wore a nine-yard sari and she tucked the pleats in around her waist. She was very house-proud. She was always in a hurry but she really looked after her family well.

The children in the chawl would often sit around eating kurmura and channe, puffed rice and gram.

'Aai, I'd like some kurmura too,' Nanda would insist. 'Give me two paise.'

'Baba, we can't afford such things. Where am I going to get two paise from? Go in now. Go on in.'

And she would drive Nanda into their house and shut the door tight. After ten minutes or so, Nanda would emerge, wiping his mouth.

'Hey, Nanda,' we would call, 'got your kurmura?'

'Nope.'

'Then what you been eating?'

'Rawa laddoos.'

When I got married, Nanda's Mum gave me an apple-shaped silver kumkum box and a silver rosewater sprinkler. She also hosted my *kelvan*—a lunch served to friends before the marriage. A woman who did not stir from her home and whose motto was '*Where I live, that's my world and what I can see, that's my universe*' trotted off to America. No doubt to feast on rawa laddoos.

Chaudhuri-tai was a loving woman. Because she came from a Brahmakshatriya world, her way of speaking was different. Her home was full of expensive objects. There were three Chaudhuris: Tai, her husband and son Dayanath. Even though she was thin she would dress up well and maintain her appearance. Her son was in charge of the production and administration of the Gandharva Natak Company. He was a brilliant electrician too. Chaudhuri-Tai was a carbon copy of Bal Gandharva. She imitated his clothes, his mannerisms, everything. When she went out, she wore a stole, as Brahmandkarbai did.

The chawl in the front housed a lecher. He had devised a rather neat if disgusting trick. He spread it about that he was an astrologer of some renown. He then trapped the naive women who came to consult him. In this he was assisted by his wife. She would tell people, especially women who would naturally trust her, of her husband's skill in reading the stars and boast of his occult knowledge. They would be lured into his presence and there he would be, lying on a cot, resplendent in shining white lungi, kurta and stole. On his forehead and his earlobes, sandalwood paste and lampblack. Around his neck, any number of chains.

When I began to work in theatre, this man tried to draw me into his coils. He sent his wife over with an expensive sari. I was out at rehearsal. My mother told me that the sari had been delivered and I was invited over. I sprang up, took the sari and went to the 'astrologer'. He saw me and in dulcet tones, invited me in. 'Babi, you've just started to work in theatre. Your future is bright, that much is sure. But if you bring me your birth chart, I could check if Saturn is…'

'There's your sari,' I said and threw it on the bed. 'I want none of it and I would advise you not to try any of this again. Which leaves the question about my stars. If I straighten you out, Shani Dev would probably bless me.'

I walked out. Neither Saturn nor the 'astrologer' got in my way after that.

*

Ramji Purushottam Chawl had its fair share of children. Every evening the compound would be full of children playing tip-cat, kho-kho or catch. When the lights went on the mothers of the chawl would begin to call, 'Come on now, get in here. You've played enough. Your Anna is here too.'

'Anna' was father. So was Appa, Tatya, Nana, Baba, all names for the fatherlog.

Skipping and *sagargote* (where you place some seeds on the back of your hand and flip them up and try to catch them in your palm and back again) were the girls' favourite games. On holidays and Sundays, we would play *sagargote*. The lunch break was given over to this game. If it had been an Olympic sport, Kashi and I would have vied for top honours. I believe that playing this keeps your mind focussed, your brain becomes alert and quick decision-making is aided.

On festival days such as Ganpati-Gauri, Dassehra and Navratri, the temple courtyard would be filled with children playing *fugdi* (where you linked hands with another and spun, each relying on the other's support) or *zhimma* (where you danced in a circle and clapped in time). It was a fabulous outdoor spectacle. When the young women wearing their *parkar-polkas* with beautiful borders began to dance, it seemed as if a series of yellow, green and jamun-purple fountains were playing. In reality, games like *akkabaichya kombda* (in which you squatted like a rooster, crossed one leg over the other knee and then jumped), *fugdi* and *zhimma* were forms of physical exercise.

There were no women's groups in those days. A haldi-koonkoo or festivals like Mangalagour or Navratri became events in the calendar of women. Caste was no bar. In the front chawl, a bangle-maker's wife, a Kasare, would be invited to a haldi-koonkoo too. These were fun-filled, laughter-soaked events, replete with jokes and riddles and much gossip. If there was a woman with a good voice she might give us a rendition of *Upvan gaat kokila* (The nightingale sings in the forest), or *Bajaao, bajaao, Murli* (Lord Krishna, play on your flute) to much applause. These were times when women could forget the workaday world and have fun for a little while.

Aai had a lovely voice. She would sing bhajans in her crystal-clear voice. She knew many *abhang*s and *ovi*s by heart. One of them ran like this:

Marzi Devachi Devachi
Mandmati durbuddhi
Marzi Devachi Devachi
Manaath yete haati-ghode.
Paalkhit baisave
Devajichya manaat
Hyaala paayi chaalvave
Marzi Devachi Devachi...

Such is God's Will
He ignores me still
Such is God's Will
I dream of elephants and horses
To sit in fine palanquins
Such is God's Will
I'm walking still
Such is God's Will

After work, she would go to the Ganpati Temple at Phadkewadi, near our home, and sing bhajans. One of them was:

Uthi Gopalji
Jaai dhenukade
Pahati Sowgandi
Vaat tujhi
Uthi Purushottama
Vaat paahi Rama

Wake up, Gopalji
Go to the cows
Your friends
Are waiting for you
Get up, Purushottama
Rama awaits you

When I heard this dawn aarti in her voice, my heart would melt. She sang in a pure soulful way, a reflection of a clear, untrammelled mind, full of devotion. Chaudhuri-Tai, Nanda's Mum and many others would plead with her to sing. And then she would sing a special bhajan: *Man paapi bhoola, kaun is-se samjhaaye* (My sinful mind neglects You/Who will set it straight?) from V Shantaram's *Aadmi* and *Aadhi beej ekle* (First, there was a single seed) from *Sant Tukaram*, both from the Prabhat Film Company's repertoire.

Nanda's maternal grandmother would sometimes come to stay with them. She knew some lovely songs.

Kasaa zhaalo mi gharzaavai
Keli aahe bhali punyaai
Kasaa zhaalo mi gharzaavai
Saasoone dili maj baayko
Ti ek dolyaane futki
Rangaane kaali shaai
Kasaa zhaalo mi gharzaavai

How did I come to live in my father-in-law's home?
It must be the good I did in a previous life
How did I come to live in my father-in-law's home?
My mother-in-law gave me a wife
She has only one eye
She's as black as ink
How did I come to live in my father-in-law's home?

Another one went:

Tuzhi maazhi jodi sakhaye,
Julel ka, saang ga.
Tuzhya paayi naazuk vahaana
Maazhya khadaavanchi daina
Julel ka, saang ga.

How will we make a match of it?
Do you think we can make it work?
Your feet have the finest sandals
My footwear is tattered and torn
Do you think we can make it work?

With Nanda's Mum keeping the rhythm by clapping, Nanda's grandmother sang this song and all the women couldn't stop laughing. She made a little too much of the feast of Ekadashi. On the whole, people have the habit of boasting about the fasts they keep. But this song was a prick to the inflated egos of those who pride themselves on their fasts:

Kadkadit nirjala
Ekadashi aaj mala
Aana mhane saabudaane
Soonth, saakhar, kaalwa mhane,
Oon oon khichdi, soone

Ghaali kutooni daane tyaala
Kadkadit nirjala
Ekadashi aaj mala

With not even a drop of water
I must keep my Ekadashi fast
Bring me some tapioca
Mix some ginger and sugar too
Now, daughter-in-law, some warm khichdi
Grind some groundnuts into it too
With not even a drop of water
I must fast for Ekadashi

In my childhood I also learned some nonsense songs by heart. Who had written these songs and how old they are, no one knows. They have been transmitted over generations by word of mouth. They are still being sung and chanted. Their words are always simple and a bit random. These songs give wings to a child's imagination. Take this one:

Kone re to?
Bhaamtewala.
Khaatos kaay?
Bhaajipaala.
Nijtos kuthe re?
Chulimaage
Baayko kuthe re?
Palangaavar
Tu nijaave
Laatha maarte
Tu maaraave
Baaher kaadte

Who's that man?
A silly old ass
What does he eat?
Just green grass
Where does he sleep?
In the coalshed
Where is his wife?
On the featherbed
Lie down near her
And she'll clout
Hit her
And she'll throw you out

About twenty-four years ago, *Aathvanithlya Kavita* (Poems from Memory) was published in four parts and they brought my schooldays back as the first rain showers always do. All these poems, which we learned at school, the devotional poems of Sant Ramdas for instance, became a part of everyday life. Poems and songs like '*Padoon aazaari, mouj heech vaate bhaari*' (It's fun to be sick, you get pampered) and '*Shraavanmaasi harsh maansi*' (In the month of Shraavan, I'm full of joy) and '*Gaai paanyaavar kaay mhanooni aalya*?' (Why these tears in your eyes?) and '*Aanandi aanand gade, ikde, tikde, chohikade*' (Joy everywhere, here, there, all around') and '*Thor tujhe upkaar*' (How great are your favours to me) and '*Khabardaar zar taach maarooni*' (Just you try and get ahead of me and see what happens) made our childhood magical.

'*Everywhere, these poems bloomed like peepul trees of memory...*' Or so the publisher has it on the cover of the books. True. The songs and poems and rhymes of our childhood had become a part of our lives.

You will remember that my elder sister's name was Kashi. So you can imagine how wonderful it was for Babu and me when we came across this poem, '*Dussehra san mota*' (Dussehra is an important festival). The first lines of the poem go:

> *Sone lootooni saayankaali Moroo paratuni aala*
> *Baheen Kashi daari yeooni ovaala mag tyaala*
> *Dasra san mota—naahi aananda tota.*
>
> (At Dussehra, the leaves of the apta tree are exchanged between friends and relatives, as auspicious tokens. They are accepted as representations of gold. Moroo has just finished this ritual and returned home where his sister, Kashi, is waiting at the door to welcome him with an aarti. Dussehra is a great festival with no shortfall of joy.)

When guests came over, parents would tell their children, 'Come, recite a poem for our guests.' The children would recite, with 'actions' to match. Schools also had recitation programmes. After many years, when English-medium schools became the rage, these Marathi poems gave way to 'Rain, rain, go away' and Bandu became Little Johnny.

My mother's education had been left incomplete but she could read well. *Smritichitre* by Laxmibai Tilak was her favourite book. She knew many of the devotional compositions of Bahinabai, Tukaram Maharaj, Sant Eknath and Sant Ramdev by heart. She also had a copy of Govindragraj's poems: *Vaagvaijayanti*.

During Ganpati, there were singing programmes at

a number of locations. In Benham Hall Lane, Hirabai Badodekar would sing while Gangoobai Hangal would sing at Khetwadi. The aficionados were spoiled for choice. Kesarbai Kerkar would sing in the homes of the rich. A select gathering of connoisseurs would gather to hear her. She too lived in Gamdevi at the time. We reaped the benefit of living so close. There Kesarbai Bandodkar (Jyotsnabai Bhole's elder sister and the painter Prafulla Dahanukar's mother) lived in Aarab House. Their home saw many artistes come and go.

Radio was very young, hardly eight to ten years old. It was amusing then, a novelty. There were few radios in people's homes. And so to listen to the radio meant you sat down and cleared your mind and paid it your full attention. This was not our way in the Ramji Purushottam Chawl. We were in the habit of chatting, laughing and talking to good glory all at once; even the radios would have stuck their fingers in their ears for a respite from our giggles and gossip.

Children our age were fascinated by the sounds we heard in our area. In the first watch of the morning, a Muslim bread vendor would come to our chawl. In his basket, he would have dozens of pao, large and small, still warm from the oven. When we heard his rooster-like call, 'Cooo-cooo-coo,' we would rush out to surround him. His cry would get even more enthusiastic.

At one anna for a pao and two annas for an egg, he did a good business. Every two or two-and-a-half months, a man came from Belgaum to sell toop (ghee or clarified butter). He wore a dhotar that stopped short at the knees, a jacket and on his head, a greasy topi. He would call out the word 'toop' in a number of tones and ways, sometimes making it 'Thyop' and sometimes 'Thoooooop' and sometimes 'Th…th…thoop' and sometimes 'Thope' but it was always very good ghee.

Once the Ganpati season had begun, we would practise a dance called baalye. We would form a circle and turn and clap in front of Gauri. The children would get to watch this extremely attractive dance form every year. These days baalye has taken on an entirely different form. Ghunghroos and the rhythm of the dholki formed its very heartbeat. Baalya is also the name of a Konkan community These Baalyas served Mumbai well for many years. They were honest and god-fearing. They were ever-ready to work. We had Narayan at our house. His salary was about three and a half rupees. He worked in ten or twelve homes, washing the vessels and clothes. He was very good at what he did. The copper vessels shone like mirrors when he was done. He was a man of few words. When he went to the village, he would ask for two or three rupees. Aai would give it willingly. In later years many Gujaratis settled in the area and the baalyas raised their wages.

The police and the municipality workers would make announcements that concerned us using a hailer, a bhonga. 'Use water carefully, there will be a shortage of water tomorrow. Tomorrrow morning there will be no water. The pipes are being repaired,' a municipal worker would shout as he walked down the street. Everyone would then gather in the front chawl. Films were also advertised in the same way on a hand cart. Posters would be affixed on both the sides of a handcart and in a shrill voice, the announcement, 'Don't forget, from tomorrow, at the Roxy,

Ashok Kumar in *Kismet*'. Vessel tinners, especially those who did brass vessels, would also advertise their presence.

But most interesting of all was the Chinese sweaterwalla[6]. When he came to the chawl we knew that winter was not far away. He would come bearing sweaters and mufflers of many a shape, design, size and colour. He was very fond of pickle. He was mad for all kinds of pickle. If you gave him two small bottles of mango and lime pickle, he would give you two thick sweaters. Two chappatis and some murabba in a plate equalled one free muffler. This meant that when the Chinese sweaterwalla arrived, the residents of the chawl found their mouths watering.

Our school had a Pathan guard. It so happened that the mother of one of my classmates came to school to pay the fees. She had really slapped on the powder. 'How much powder she's put on!' I said or something of the sort. Really, I had no business saying that. It was her face. Her powder too. But it was not the age to think logically. When her daughter told her what I said, she got angry and slapped me on the face, grabbed her daughter and marched off. I sat on the steps, weeping. The Pathan noticed. He asked what had happened. When I told him, he said, '*Tum darne ka vaasta naahin beti, hum dekhta haai*.' ('Don't you fear, little one. Lemme take care of things.')

Some days later, the woman came to school for something else altogether. Really speaking, she must have forgotten the whole incident. But the Pathan caught her at the door. 'You got angry, fine. But you shouldof explained

---

[6]It is possible that he was a Tibetan.

things to her. She's a wee thing. How couldja hit her? And one more thing: you do put on too much powder. There. I've said it. Now what you going to do? Hit me too?'

Now the poor lady needed some more powder. If all this had gone to Varubai Padhye's ears and from there to my mother's, I would not have been spared but the Pathan settled the matter.

Many years later I saw Bimal Roy's exquisite film, *Cabuliwallah*, based on the Rabindranath Tagore story and I thought of that hefty but extraordinarily loving Pathan. The Pathan and the Chinese sweaterwalla both told me that a bigger world outside the Ramji Purushottam Chawl existed. This realization grew slowly as the years passed.

Right in front of the chawl was a narrow gully. It led to Khotachiwadi. This is one of Mumbai's jewels. Many of the houses belonged to Christians. It was clean and peaceful. The houses were built in the Portuguese style. One felt as if one had stumbled into a Goan village. In the middle of the wadi was a small shrine to Mother Mary. There was also a club for the residents of the area. There the men played billiards in the evening. From many of the houses came the sounds of Western music.

At one point in time, the Mumbai Municipality decided to change the name of Khotachiwadi. Khotachiwadi exploded. The Christian community, known for its '*socegado*'—its fun-loving and peaceable nature—came out on the streets. They declared that generations had been born and lived in a place called Khotachiwadi and generations to come would die there or they'd know the reason why. They would not let the name, which was how everyone knew the area, be wiped out. The Mahapalika backed down.

Victorious, the Christian community went back to its *socegado* ways. There were large settlements of Christians around the Metro Cinema and Dhobi Talao and Chira Bazaar and further out at Colaba. Those who came from Goa went there to find homes. There were even Goan Christian restaurants in some of the buildings around Dhobi Talao. There were also some lodging houses. Other Christians lived in Mahim and Bandra. That was as far as our knowledge went.

Behind the chawl was Hurkisondas Hospital. Further on was a Parsi Baug. I do not know if it is still there. The buildings were three or four storeys and were all dull yellow. The surrounding area was clean as were the courtyards. It was so quiet that you could not help but wonder whether anybody was at home at all. There were also baugs at Colaba and, at Babulnath, some beautiful Parsi bungalows.

The Parsis were rich and enterprising. They loved cars and drove around in Buicks, Morrises and Baby Austins. Their wives wore georgette saris and blouses without sleeves. Their plump fair children always caught the eye. There was a Parsi marriage hall close to Charni Road Station. Their children would have their navjotes (initiation ceremonies) there too. The marriages that took place were fantastic: fairy lights would be hung up on the trees; a Parsi or Christian band would be tuning up to play Western music; the well-dressed guests would be getting out of cars…it was all rather beautiful to watch. There would always be a bunch of onlookers standing on the road and gawping at a rich family's celebrations. However, there was never any ugly show of wealth either.

They would have dinner on plantain leaves. Guests would be served in rows. We had heard that they held rangoli and sandalwood in the highest respect. They also had a huge affection for dogs. Many, many years ago, I think it would be about a hundred or a hundred and twenty-five years ago, a small incident in which someone threw a stone at a dog sparked off a riot between Parsis and Muslims[7]. This, some say, was the first full-scale riot in Mumbai.

It was in 1935 that *Jawaani ki Hawa*, produced by Bombay Talkies, was released. I was eight years old then. Parsi society was convulsed. This was because the music director of the film was Saraswati Devi. She was a Parsi. Her real name was Khurshid Minocher Homji. That a Parsi girl should go into films made the Parsis very angry. They came out on to the streets. There were riots in Grant Road and Lamington Road even as the leaders of the community, the police and the owners of Bombay Talkies were trying to sort things out.

In truth, at that time, there was a strong connection between Parsis and cinema. Many rich Parsis had invested

---

[7]*In Giants of Immortality; World's Smallest Minority: Its Past and Present (Briefly Told)* S H Jhabvala says: '...in 1876 a dog was supposedly killed by a Muslim and its carcase was thrown near a Hindu temple. A riot was the consequence. The dog is considered to be a sacred animal by the Parsees, its services being utilized for *Sag-Deed* (gaze of the dead body by the dog before removing the corpse to the Towers of Silence) and the Parsees joined the Hindus in opposition to the Muslim offence. The riot spread like wildfire and Sir Jamsetjeee Jeejeebhoy and other elders with Sir Jagannath Shankarsett and Sir Mangaldas Nathubhai on the Hindu side settled it with Government assistance after much serious blood-shed and loss of property.'

in the motion pictures. Ardeshir Irani was one of cinema's biggest names. J B H Wadia, Homi Wadia and Sohrab Modi were all names to conjure with. But the Parsis felt that it was not right for their womenfolk to go into cinema. In some ways, they were quite conservative. They were deeply concerned about their religious traditions and social mores and so one never saw Parsi women on the screen.

Saraswati Devi was a talented music director. She had studied music at Lucknow's famous Bhatkhande Music College. Her sister had taken the name of Chandra Prabha for a while. She too had worked in a film. Both of them were very good at music. They were known as the Homji sisters. Saraswati Devi had composed some simple tunes for *Jawaani ki Hawa*. Devika Rani was the heroine of the film. She was beautiful but she was not a good singer and so the tunes had to be kept simple.

Next came *Achhut Kanya* (The Untouchable Girl). In this film, the Ashok Kumar and Devika Rani duet *Main ban ki chidiya banke sang doloon re* (Let me turn into a sparrow in the jungle and we can live it up) became a big hit. Similarly, '*Main to Dilli se dulhan laaye re, Oh Babuji*' (I've got me a bride from Delhi, my good sir) from *Jhoola* was extremely popular. Saraswati Devi's name was on everyone's lips. My favourite, if anyone were to ask me, of Saraswati Devi's oeuvre was *Sooni padi re sitar Meera ke jeevan ki* (Meera's life has been devastated; her sitar is silent).

How I have wandered. I started talking about the communities of Bombay and have ended up with Saraswati Devi's music but that is what happens when you follow the will-o'-the-wisp of memory. One thing leads to another and then to a third and fourth. Memories come one after the other, like raindrops in a shower…

We were talking about music. All three of us loved the songs of the New Theatres Film Company. '*Chale pavan ki chaal jag mein chale pavan ki chaal*' (The wind blows through the world, how it blows), '*Dole hriday ki naiyya*' (My heart rocks like a boat on stormy seas), '*Ik bangla bane nyaura*' (I'll build a unique house for you), '*Kahoon kya aas niraas bhayi*' (Shall I speak of my disappointments in love?), '*Yeh duniya ek Toofan Mail*', (The world is a speeding train, a Toofan Mail) '*Kisne khel rachaaya*' (Who put on this play?), '*Babul mora naihar chhooto ri jaaye*' (As I leave my father's home) were always on our lips. These songs were based on Bengali tunes. In later years S D Burman and Hemant Kumar began to become popular. I also remember New Theatre's Pankaj Mullick and Raichandra Boral.

My brother loved the songs of K C Dey (Manna Dey's uncle) and Saigal. *Do naina matwaare tihaare hum par julm kare* (Your beautiful eyes savage my heart), *Duniya rang rangeeli baba* (The world is a spectacular place). When Babu began singing these songs an unnameable ache filled the mind. We loved Saigal. His voice was exceptionally sweet and deeply expressive of pain. His '*Main kya jaanoo kya jaadoo hai*' (What magic is this?) is immortal. I loved his songs. 'Loved' is incorrect. I still love them. I can still listen to them. Just as the songs of the saints are outside time and will never grow stale or old, so Saigal's songs remain evergreen.

Prabhat's songs appealed to the heart. The company's

music directors experimented with the tunes, orchestration and composition. The credit for this must go to Keshavrao Bhole and Master Krushnarao Phulambrikar. These two talented music directors gave Prabhat its distinctive sound by blending the traditional and the new. The Prabhat songs were both musical and meaningful. In songs like *Ek tatv naam dhrud dhari manaa Harisi karuna yeil tujhi* (Commit yourself to the name of God and He will have mercy on you), *Aadhi beej ekle, Mann paapi bhola kaun is-se samjhaaye,* (you can hear a thousand years of unbroken cultural tradition, handed down from generation to generation).

The unforgettable films made by these two companies had a great impact on my generation. For us actors like Saigal, Pramathesh Barua, Kananbala, Uma Shashi and Pahadi Sanyal were like stars in the sky. Most people in Marathi society thought of the actors in Prabhat's films as relatives: Shahu Modak, Shanta Apte, Shanta Hublikar, Keshavrao Date, and Baby Vaasanti.

Bombay Talkies films were full of masala and entertainment. This was a cinema from Mumbai for Mumbai audiences. Himashu Rai, the founder, had taken stock of the many castes, communities and linguistic groups, the *athrapagad jaatis*[8] that made the city their home and figured out their lowest common denominator. He and director Sashadhar Mukherjee had come up with a cinema for them. Rai's wife, Devika Rani was the leading lady of their films. Her fans were legion. It was said that

---

[8]Literally 'eighteen ways of wearing a turban', each representing a different community.

Jawaharlal Nehru had sent her a congratulatory note after seeing *Achhut Kanya*. She brought to mind the Atre line, '*Swargaatlya paryaana ke vastragaal karooni/Ramaneeya deha vidheene rachila ticha chhabela*' (All the graces of the heavenly dancers were distilled in the form of this one woman.) There was a dignity in her beauty. Durga Khote also had this ability: to offer the gift of her beauty with dignity. Devika Rani was a flower in bud; Durga Khote was in full bloom.

Ashok Kumar was the leading man. I thought he looked rather juvenile in *Achhut Kanya*. But in the next ten years, he got his act together and emerged as a seasoned actor. I did not see *Achhut Kanya* when it was released; I was too young to be allowed to go to the movies. I saw it much later. But Babu and I did see *Bandhan*, *Kangan* and *Jhoola* at the Roxy Cinema. This was where the Bombay Talkies films were released. Ashok Kumar and Leela Chitnis became a star pair. Ashok Kumar's most successful film was *Kismet*, where he played a criminal. Babu and I saw that at the Roxy too. The story had pace; the songs were hugely successful. Anil Biswas had composed the music for *Kismet*. *Dheere dheere aa re baadal, dheere dheere aa re, mera bulbul so raha hai, shor na machaa*, (My nightingale sleeps, do not disturb her, O clouds, float gently by), a song by Ashok Kumar, became a great favourite with audiences. Kavi Pandit Pradeep's '*Door hato eh duniyawaalon, Hindostan hamaara hai*' (Stand away, O worldly ones, Hindustan is ours) caused a wave of enthusiasm to sweep over the city. The struggle for independence was coming to a head.

The people had had enough of British rule. The colonial overlords could also see the end coming. In this situation, the lyrics seemed incendiary.

Yahaan hamaara Taj Mahal hai
Aur Qutb Minaara hai
Yahaan hamaare mandir-masjid
Sikhon ka Gurdwara hai.
Is dharti pe kadam badhaana
Atyachaar tumhaara hai.
Door hato eh duniyawaalon
Hindustan hamaara hai
Aaj Himalaya ki chotise
Phir humne lalkaara hai
Door hato eh duniyawaalon
Hindustan hamaara hai.

Here our Taj Mahal stands
Here is our Qutb Minara
Here our temples and our mosques
Here the Sikh Gurudwara
For you to set foot on this soil
Is to violate holy lands
Stay away, O wordly wise
Ours is Hindustan
From the heights of the Himalaya
We challenge you this day
Stay away, O wordly wise
Hindustan is ours

The government of Mumbai sent representatives to Sashadhar Mukherjee and Kavi Pradeep to inquire into the exact meaning of the song. A huge discussion followed. It was the time of the Second World War. Rumour had it that India would also be attacked. The song was aimed, Sashadhar maintained, at Stalin, Hitler and Japan. It was not an anti-colonial song. This reassured the government and audiences at the Roxy were once more regaled with 'Door hato…' Once it was over, the reel would be rewound and the song would be played five or six times before the rest of the film could continue.

About twenty-two years after *Kismet*, India once again faced difficult times when China had attacked India. At this time, it was a song that bound the nation together; and once again it was Kavi Pradeep who wrote it: '*Ai mere watan ke logon*' (O people of my land). It was put to music by C Ramachandra and Lata Mangeshkar lent her ethereal voice to it. The song became immortal. Music has magic in it. It draws people together. It stays with you long after other things have departed. At every rite of passage, in happiness and in woe, music follows us. Music helps us through times of trouble. It has charms to soothe the beast or set the heart aflame. People come together and drift apart again but a song in your heart never leaves you. Human relationships may be temporary but a song stays with you, as your shadow does.

All the residents of the Ramji Purushottam Chawl had seen bioscope shows but they were not very interested in cinema. The films of Prabhat were, however, particularly popular: *Sant Tukaram* and *Sant Dnyaneshwar*, for instance. There were special 'zenana' shows for women. Otherwise, women were only occasional viewers of Pauranic films. Theatre was also popular. It was a mark of cultural sophistication to see Bal Gandharva's plays. The plays by Atre and Mama Warerkar were also popular. Attending public lectures was another tradition. Near the Opera House was the Blavatsky Hall and there was the famous Jinnah Hall at Lamington Road or the Shantaram

Chawl at Girgaon. At any of these places one might hear Acharya Atre, Barrister Jaykar, Sarojini Naidu or Sardar Vitthalbhai Patel speaking.

People also loved reading. There were popular weeklies and monthly magazines such as *Chitra*, *Vasundhara* and *Mouj* which had many faithful readers. From time to time these days one hears of television serials that have been discontinued and people wonder why; in those days, a magazine would suddenly stop and we would wonder why.

After a period of a few months, the same publisher would start another magazine with another name. *Dhanurdhaari* was a very popular magazine because of Vasant Ladoba Mhapankar's astrology column. He was a celebrity astrologer in those days. Baburao Arnalkar was no less famous. His books were sold for four annas. The atmosphere Arnalkar conjured up was vastly romantic, mystery stories for the masses. He was very skilful at building up atmosphere: mist swathed the scenery and snow often fell. It seemed as if the Black Mountain had left Europe and had risen in Girgaon; and this we thought was a very fine thing. For Arnalkar had a way of erasing the line between fiction and fact. His four-anna series took up a great deal of space in our fantasy world.

But it was Mary Evans or Fearless Nadia who ruled the hearts of the masses. I saw one film starring her: *Hunterwaali* at the Super Cinema, Grant Road. What Nadia got up to on the screen was nothing short of the miraculous. She beat up strong men and tossed them around as if they were dolls. She would spring from trains and swing from chandeliers. She would leap on to a horse and ride off into the sunset. The audiences were astounded by her antics but they were also completely enthralled by them. Most of her fans were working-class men. The names of her films were also intriguing: *Diamond Queen*, *Miss Frontier Mail*, *Lootera Lalna* (The Lovable Thief), *Rolls Royce ki Beti* (Daughter of Rolls Royce).

I did not see *Rolls Royce ki Beti* myself but an incident from the film had become famous. In it, Nadia starts her car with a single kick. A literal-minded filmgoer wrote to *Film India* and other film monthly magazines to say that if Nadia were to sell her Rolls Royce, she would get a fine price for in this time of rationing, is it not a wonderful thing that it starts with a single kick. *Film India*'s editor Baburao Patel replied: 'One kick from Nadia and J B H Wadia has to count out Rs 1500.' There was another discussion that took up a lot of time and attention from film fans. Who was the highest paid film star? Was it Miss Madhuri? Or Sulochana (who had been born Ruby Meyers)? Or Miss Nadia?

Cinema was becoming an ever-more powerful medium by the day and yet society had not made up its mind about how to deal with it. By the time the Second World War began, there was no doubting its power. The films made by New Theatres and Prabhat were rich in content and were loved by the people. But around 1940, the cinema of Lahore came to Mumbai. This was a melodramatic cinema, with titillating songs, strapping men and sumptuous women. The pallid middle-class man began to lose sleep over these images. And there developed the idea that cinema was all bad things put together but this was a minority opinion among a diminishing class of people. Otherwise the average Marathi was rather pleased that people like V Shantaram, Master Vinayak, Bhalji Pendharkar, Durga Khote, Leela Chitnis, Shanta Apte, Vanamala and Shobhana Samarth had become stars. However, it was still difficult for anyone from the film industry to find housing in 'respectable' areas like Dadar or Girgaon. Here cinema people were held to be *chhangi-bhangi chhatisrangi*—people of dubious morals and improper behaviour. No one wanted them as neighbours. 'A *kalavant* (actress) is fine on stage and in the night. But when she's cleaning her teeth with tobacco in the morning? Who needs such a sight?' went a common saying. In other words: we want cinema but we don't want to have anything to do with those who make it, or so society thought.

That reminds me of something that happened not so long ago. In a rather intoxicated state, Salman Khan is said to have gone to the building in which Aishwarya Rai lived and shouted her name loudly. This happened three or four times and the residents of the building began to object. They wanted a stay order put on Salman Khan and so the matter ended up with the police. And once again, the residents began to say that it was Aishwarya Rai's presence in the building that was causing the problem. At least, that is what one read in the press. In our days, there were no public scandals like this one.

There must have been 'goings on' in the film world but these affairs did not reach the ears of the ordinary citizen. Perhaps society had some basic values. The narrative of the nation was in the hands of men like Gandhi, Nehru, Patel and Subhash Chandra Bose. This was also echoed in the film world. Actors tried to behave with dignity. It was not their habit to allow their private lives to become the material of street gossip. For instance it was well known that Sardar Chandulal Shah was sweet on Miss Gohar. He was the head of Ranjit Movietone and she was a leading lady of the cinema but I do not remember either of them ever giving an interview about their private lives. Nor do I remember the newspapers carrying such interviews. Cinema did not show up on the radar of the mainstream press. Some film magazines did come out on a monthly basis but there was no habit of bringing them home to read. *Film India* was one of the classy magazines of the time. But it was also very expensive. It cost fifteen to twenty rupees. *Chitra* and *Vasundhara* were other monthlies in which M G Rangnekar would sometimes write about cinema. Badri Kanchwalla also brought out a film magazine in Gujarati. Once Shanta Apte caused a storm. It so happened that Baburao Patel wrote a particularly scathing review of her performance in a film. Shanta Apte was offended. It is said that she took a fine stick and marched to the *Film India* office and gave him a resounding beating. The film world lacks such women of violent temper but even Shantabai did not offer a repeat performance. Nor did she ever give as fine a performance as she did in *Kunku*.

In R G Gadkari's play *Ekach pyaala* (Just one glassful) there is a famous speech given by Taliram. I no longer remember the words but I do remember the sense of one section. He says that there is a fine line of fire, an imaginary line, that separates viewer from actor. This line must not be crossed by either. The actors and actresses of our time seemed to be instinctively aware of this. They did not appear much in public. You would not see them at 'functions' or 'events'. They had their own world, it seemed. Even their homes were in far-off places such as Colaba or Marine Drive or Bandra and Chembur. The studios were in Dadar or Parel. But to get entry into those studios was tantamount to crossing the seven seas, the seven mountains and the seven deserts. Within these safe confines, they could maintain an air of mystery. That also fed their viewers' curiosity about them.

I think my mother had the last word on the subject of cinema. She had become aware that the craze for cinema was not going to abate and so she had developed her own formula for dealing with it. This was summed up in the phrase: Set up the gramophone but don't play the music. Confused? Let me explain. At the home of a certain Konkani Muslim, a wedding was imminent. It was a large family and all the members had arrived. The younger generation wanted a gramophone to play music. The older generation opposed the idea and so eventually the matter was taken to the reigning patriarch of the family, a very old man. He listened patiently to the arguments on both sides and then gave his decision. The young people might bring a gramophone to the wedding but no music would be played on it.

That was my mother's attitude to cinema.

When we went to see a film, she did not try to stop us nor did she accuse us of foolishness. But once in a while, she would tell us what she thought of the whole thing: 'Arré, what's that saineema (for her own peculiar reasons she chose to call it that) all about? There's no-o-thing in it. They just take some money from you and show you some rubbish in return.' She might well have been talking about the cinema of today.

As an art form, cinema has completed a hundred years as I write but the films of today seem like the last gasp of a centenarian. The music and stories seem pallid and thin compared to the films I saw as a child. Often it does not seem as if there is a story to tell at all. The songs have no discernible melody. I must confess here that I am a fan of the cinema of V Shantaram, Mehboob Khan, Bimal Roy, Mahesh Kaul, Raj Kapoor, Hrishikesh Mukherjee and Gulzar. These directors were adept at exposition; they created minor characters around their central protagonists but gave each one nuances that embellished the storyline. This also enriched the viewers' experience of the diversity of humanity. Think about actors like Durga Khote, Motilal, Lalita Pawar, Kanhaiyalal, Sulochana Bai, Dhumal, Pran, Om Prakash, Rehman, Sapru, Shashikala, Helen, Tun Tun, Mehmood and Johnny Walker, Achla Sachdev. In *Waqt*, I still remember Achla Sachdev in a song, '*Ae mere zohrajabeen, tujhe maloom nahin*', (My beloved, you have no idea how beautiful you still are) and how sweetly she flirted with Balraj Sahni. These are all memorable figures. In truth, many of these actors who played supporting roles were much more talented than the stars.

Good films still come out but they seem few and far between. Of the present lot, I have enjoyed films like *Jodha Akbar*, *A Wednesday*, *Kahaani* and *Lagaan*. Watching one of them is like dipping your feet into a cold stream after walking barefoot for miles in the noonday sun. Producers and directors these days pay scant attention to the music of their films. Songs are the life of our cinema. Audiences may forget the names of films or the actors or actresses involved but they do not forget the songs they love. Today all the songs sound the same. Perhaps it is because the songs do not spring from the specific musical imagination of the music director. In the past every music director had his own distinctive 'sound'. You could not mistake an Annasahib Chitalkar song for a Naushad song; Anil Biswas had his own style; Shankar-Jaikishen had their own signature.

There also seems to be a lot of shouting going on in today's music. The hero will be standing right next to the heroine but for some reason he still seems to find it necessary to shout in her ears. One begins to wonder if she is supposed to be a little deaf. But then I often wonder whether it is I who am losing my hearing. Perhaps it is because of my increasing years but could it not also be that my ears are endangered by this cacophony? Mohammed Rafi's *Aap ke haseen rukh pe aaj naya noor hai, mera dil machal gaya to mera kya qasoor hai* (There's a new light in your face today/If my heart misses a beat, who can blame it?) from *Bahaarein Phir Bhi Aayegi* is sung in such a smooth and velvety voice. To listen to Talat Mehmood's *Yeh hawa, yeh raat, yeh chandni, teri ik adaa pe nisaar hai* (I would sacrifice this night, this breeze and this moonlight for a single glance from you) from *Sangdil* (music director: Sajjid Hussain) is to have one's heart caressed by feathers. Lata Mangeshkar's *Lag jaa gale ke phir haseen raat ho na ho* (Take me in your arms for who knows about tomorrow?) from *Woh Kaun Thi?* for music director O P Nayyar or Asha Bhosle's *Chhota-sa balma akhiyan neend churaaye le gayo* (My young lover has stolen the sleep from my eyes) from *Jaal* for music director Hemant Kumar, are beautiful and delicate songs. When I hear these songs, they seem new all over again even though they are forty to fifty years old. They are still popular with listeners. On television shows such as *Sa Re Ga Ma Pa*, the compositions of Shankar-Jaikishen, S D Burman, Madan Mohan, Roshanlal, Salil Chowdhury are still sung and received with great affection. The judges are contemporary music directors. Do they ever wonder whether their songs will stand the test of time as these have?

People say times have changed and so music has changed too. People change with the times, they say. I do not deny any of this but the question is how much have we changed? Have we begun to walk on our hands? Have babies stopped breastfeeding? Some sensibilities are eternal. Our music is eternal. The love of melody is eternal.

This is the age of technology. Because we have so many ways and means and media, the songs of Lata, Talat, Geeta Dutt, Maniktai Verma, Shobha Gurtu, Pandit Kumar Gandharva, Begum Akhtar and Kesarbai Kerkar are now within easy reach. I can listen to them whenever I choose, a great joy to me. I have wandered quite a bit. Let me come back to my own life…

My life flowed along as a leaf flows on a stream. I went to school, Babu to the Orient School. Kashi finished her matriculation and started a nursing course. I hated mathematics with its never-ending calculations of pounds, shillings and pence, its fraction times tables—one quarter is a quarter, two quarters is a half and so on—and as soon as the class began, I wished it were over. I enjoyed Marathi and History. In the afternoon break, we skipped or played *sagargote* and we hoped that the hands of the clock would slow down for us.

To us children in those days, the silver foil inside a cigarette packet was like treasure given to us by the God of Wealth. We would snip it into silvery fringes. Another pastime was to cut up coloured paper and make designs out of it. As we came home from school, we would look for empty cigarette packets, broken bits of glass and any pretty pictures. Sometimes Aai would take us to Chowpatty beach or Malabar Hill for a day trip. The edge of the sea offered many lovely things: shells, conches, pieces of mica. We were not supposed to touch mica, Aai had warned us.

Another of our games was to place small coins on the heated rails of the trams when no one was looking. It was our fond belief that no one saw us doing this. They probably did but dismissed us as stupid children and went on their way. Children have the ability to overthrow the world and its rules. That is what makes childhood so wonderful. And so we wandered through the city, our childhood a passport and a badge.

In those days, parents were not in the habit of asking their children to get ninety per cent or stand first in the examinations. Their demands were simple: go to school, study hard, return safe and in one piece, do your homework with attention. Most parents would say things like: 'Our children are not likely to join the civil services or anything like that. It's enough if they do their Matric and get stuck in somewhere, the post office maybe, or the municipality.' Even so it was a matter of pride to Marathi folk when Chintamanrao Dwarkanath Deshmukh[9] went to England and joined the Indian Civil Service.

---

[9]C D Deshmukh (1886-1982) graduated from Jesus College, Cambridge; he was the first Indian to be Governor of the Reserve Bank of India and topped the Civil Services Examination in 1918.

It was not important for a child to study a great deal, then. If he lived according to the rules and regulations of his community and had some natural intelligence, that was seen as enough. Our society seemed to be content if a child learned how to behave so as not to hurt anybody deliberately and if he could meet and mingle with all kinds of people. These thoughts were expressed in many songs, proverbs and verses that were popular at the time:

Ati kopata kaarya zaate layaala
Ati namrata paatra hote bhayaala
Ati kaam te kontehi nasaave
Pramaanamadhe sarv kaahin asaave

Too much anger and things go bad
Too gentle? They'll think you're scared
Too much of anything leaves no ease
Bring balance to your energies

The middle path was supposed to be the best. Krishnaji Narayan Athalye's poem that offered a message of moderation in all things and promised a successful and happy life was very popular. *Don't eat too much sweet, don't eat too much junk food, don't chase the new, don't be too greedy for money, don't insist on the old, don't talk too much, don't offend with silence.*

All this in one poem.

Some poets did not only offer advice but also wrapped in some stern warnings.

Kasa tula chhandach khelnyaachaa
Mauu bichhaanyaawar lolanyaachaa
Kashi tula vaatat laaj naahin
Sadaa hasaave tujla janaani

How come you're so fond of games?
How come you're always lolling?
How come you have no sense of shame?
Don't you find their laughter galling?

Another example:

Mulaano tumhi sarv ho khel soda
Manin kaalji baalga, dnyaan zoda
Asaa kaal tumhaala kaisa milel
Pudhe dukh hota tumhaala kalel

Children set aside childish games
Store up wisdom in your minds
The time you waste will never return
You will rue this in due time

Then there was '*Bikat vaat vahivaat nasaavi; dhopat marg sodu naka*' or 'Stick to the straight and narrow'. Lines from this poem would be offered as correctives to children. These included:

Durmukhlela asoo nako
Vyavahaaramadhi phasoo nako
Kadhi rikaama basoo nako

Don't sit around with a long face
Don't get fooled by the world
Don't sit idle

Or there was:

Kashtaachi bari bhaajibhaakri;
toopsaakhre choroo nako
Dili sthiti Devaane teetach maani sukh,
Kadhi vitoo naka

Better the simple food of your labour
than rich food stolen from your neighbour
Be happy where God has put you
Don't let bitterness get you

One straight-talking message offered by Sant Ramdas: '*Bare satya bola, yathatathya chaala, bahu maaniti lok yene tumhaala*' or 'Speak the truth and behave well, this is the way to earn the respect of others'. In the next lines, Sant Ramdas says something that children might not enjoy hearing:

Bahu khel khota, aalasya khota
Samastaanshi bhaandel tochi karanta.

Don't play too much; don't be too lazy
You'll do nothing if you fight with all

We did not follow his messages. We played a lot and we fought almost as much. Then we played some more and fell asleep and slept soundly.

When Aai was on night duty, Babu and I would miss her. We would miss Kashi too, who was in the Sassoon Hospital, training to be a nurse. She could only come home from Pune once a month or so. Education had given her a new self-confidence, I could see.

When Aai was at home at night, it was as if the house were filled with light. We would eat together and she would hum a song or two. '*Chindhi baandhate Draupadi Harichya botala*' (Draupadi ties a strip of cloth around Hari's finger) or '*Jaaooni saanga Shri Harila, Yashoda bhete Sudamyala*' (Go tell Shri Hari, Yashoda has met Sudama).

And sleep would steal slowly over us.

Velvet Curtains

IN THOSE DAYS, WE COOKED SIMPLE BUT TASTY FOOD. Most people ate rice with vegetables and curry. If the vegetables were cooked as paatal bhaaji—with gravy—it was not considered necessary to cook a curry as well. Treats that made me happy were rice with varan (dal) and koshimbir; or pitlabhaat, rice and a curry made out of gram flour.

We ate curds and buttermilk with our food. Sprouts were popular. Then the Second World War began and with it rationing came to Mumbai. The government provided us with rice from Brazil. The grains were round and rough and took ages to cook and it was still difficult to eat. It was during the Second World War that we Konkanis—*Kokanye, bhaat bokanye* (rice-gobblers) as we were called—began to eat wheat. This may be seen as one of Hitler's greatest achievements.

Polis[1] were rare at our home. Rice had been our staple food. On Sunday, mutton or fish sometimes made an appearance. Mutton was available at a shop near Krishna Talkies at Grant Road. It would take a long time to cook. Lunch would therefore be delayed to two or two-thirty p.m.

[1]This is the Brahmin Maharashtrian way of referring to chapattis or rotis.

At that time, we did not have cooking gas in the chawl. We cooked on mud hearths; stoves came later. We had a huge grinding stone on which all the masalas were ground either by Aai or one of the girls. The food had a great flavour to it then even though it was not elaborate fare. *Govind Gopal he doghe bandhu/ jeveet hote kadhi-bhaat limbu* (Govind and Gopal were two brothers of our time/ they ate rice with curry and lime) was a popular rhyme at the time. And truly, steaming hot rice covered with varan and a piece of lime (or lime pickle) was the best meal you could have. Rice with buttermilk and mango pickle was another great meal. Aai made wonderful bhakri, a flatbread made with jowar flour. That was comfort food for me: bhakri, leafy vegetables and buttermilk. Bliss!

We made our own laddoos out of rawa (semolina) and besan (gram flour). Savouries like sev and chiwda were also made at home. These were meant for guests and younger children. We also cooked our own sheera-pohe and thaali peeth. The aroma of thali peeth would spread through the chawl. It was with pleasure that we went visiting friends or relatives. There were many occasions for such visits. Sometimes it would be a festival or a celebration. Sometimes it would be a visit to someone ill or convalescing. One put a lot of hard work into one's relationships and didn't break off with someone on a flimsy excuse. One didn't 'part on a fart' as the saying goes. One didn't go to extremes when dealing with people. That meant you didn't get too close to people either lest you got hurt when something went wrong.

If you were offended by something or upset by something a friend or relative did, you didn't talk about it to everyone. You didn't wash your dirty linen in public. You looked after what was yours and left others to look after what was theirs. It was best to avoid those who hurt you. It was enough to assure oneself that one's behaviour was as good as one could make it. You did not bring up what was bad. Rehashing it would only damage you in the end. You tried not to think too much about the offending person and his behaviour.

These were the beliefs by which people lived. There was a wisdom in this, I think. The women of the house seemed to understand this better than the menfolk. If some friend of relative had behaved badly, the lady of the house was likely to say: 'Never mind. Let it go. Why burn over this? You did the right thing, no? That will have been recorded in God's ledger,' or something of the kind.

We were not explicitly taught these things. We absorbed them from how people behaved at home and in society. Our own uncle had driven us from our ancestral home in Adivré. Our mother came to Mumbai and blazed our trail for us. She made no mention of this to the people who visited us. And from her example, we realised that you must put behind you the hurts and disappointments of yesterday and apply yourself to the job of working today to make tomorrow better. It was on such wisdom that our society was firmly based. It also gave women the strength to go on. Later women would gain their independence through further education. My mother was largely unlettered. But she had got herself trained as a midwife and saved our family. In those days, many women began to demand an education. This has had an impact on Maharashtra's society that cannot be underestimated.

Women, in those times, had a whole host of sayings, pithy proverbs for every occasion. They were in regular use. Your grandmother might say to you, '*Aamhi kaay bai kaahi kaamache naahi. Khaayla kaal aani bhuila bhaar*' ('I'm not much use any more. I'll just eat and burden the world.') If there were a fight over some irrelevant issue, then '*Baazaaraat turi and Bhat Bhatnila maari*' (which literally means that what happens in the market makes the Brahmin beat his wife, but it signified anger which had no real reason for its existence.) When Samrath had his relatives over from the village and they overstayed their welcome, it was held to be a case of '*Bhattala dili osri and Bhatt haath-paay pasri*' or 'Give the Brahmin an inch and he takes a mile'. If a parent tired of lecturing the children who paid no attention, she or he might say, '*Nali phookli sonare, ikdoon tikdoon gele vaare*'. Again literally this meant 'The goldsmith's smelting tube is useless if it has more than one hole' for the flame will not be concentrated on the part he wants. Similarly a child who lets instruction go in through one ear and come out of the other will not benefit from it. The saying '*Bhide bhide pot vaadhe*' (Get too close and a pregnancy may come about) may sound a bit inappropriate now but '*Bheed bhikechi bahin*' (Inhibition is the sister of beggary) was much the same thing. '*Ati raag bheek maag*' suggested that too much anger might set you on the path to beggary.

There was a proverb which went: '*Naav Sonubai, haati kathilaacha vaala*' or 'She's been named after gold but poor thing/her bangles are only made of tin'. '*Chhadi laage chum chum, vidya yeii ghum ghum*' or 'Beat the child on his bum, and watch how quickly knowledge comes' was a saying that has been the undoing of many children. There was also a proverb that went '*Aaplya to baabya, dusryaacha te kaart*' or 'My poor son cannot be blamed, while yours is a devil who needs to be tamed'. But this proverb could also come back to sting your own child.

'*Ta' mhatlyaavar taak-bhaat*' or 'You only have to say "r", and he can tell you mean rice' was used to describe a smart person. We said, '*Aawla deoon kohla kaadnyaat*' to describe a person who could give an amla, a small sour fruit, and get a pumpkin in exchange. A simple hard-working woman was '*Allagharchi gaay*' or the cow of Allah's home. '*Jyaala naahi akkal, tyaachi gharoghari nakkal*' or 'The fool meets with contumely everywhere' was of course an insult. Anyone who has lived in a Mumbai chawl will understand why we often said that the walls have ears ('*Bhinteena kaan astaat*'). Likewise, '*Uchalli jeebh an laavli taalyala*' warned against speaking without thinking which might result in bankruptcy. There was another saying, '*Zhaakli mooth savva laakhaachi*' that said what you have hidden in your fist may well be worth a treasure but as soon as you open your hand everyone will know its worth.

There were also some phrases that were used to ridicule the rich and their ways. '*Mothya lokaancha, gaadga bhokaancha*' (The pot of the rich man has a hole in it) and '*Mote kule tikde jag bhule*' (The world follows the big of bottom). The rich were viewed with suspicion. It was not wrong then nor does it seem wrong now. Look at what one reads in the papers. The scams of the rich are everywhere. *Mangoo Sheth, uska bada pet* (Mangoo is a rich man but his appetite is big too) as they say in Hindi, was typical of Mumbai's attitude. You replaced the name Mangoo with that of a rich man from your area and you had your own proverb.

The songs from the theatre were also very popular. Some lines from the songs acquired the status of proverbs. For instance Master Dinanath's bright sharp voice in *Parvashta paash daivé* (Foreign rule is a noose in your destiny), singing *Asooni khaas maalik gharaacha, mhanti chor tyaala* (The owner of the house is taken as a thief) became a well-known saying as did *Kathin, kathin, kathin, kiti, purush-hriday, bai* (Oh my lady, hard, hard, hard is the heart of man). *Shrimant patichi raani mag thaat kaay toh pusta* (She's the wife of a rich man; what can one say of her style?) or *Dantajiche thane oothle, phutle doni kaan/Turlak kothe, kes rooperi, doees takkal chhaan, avghe paoonshe vaymaan* (He's lost his teeth, he's stone-deaf, his hair is silver and so scanty you could say he's bald, but this man who seeks your hand, he's not aged, he's only seventy-five years old) were lines from the play *Sharda* by G B Deval. Madhavrao Joshi's *Sangeet Municipality* had a song that was extremely popular among the people. Some lines ran thus:

Shing phunkeet gela Ingreji paanyaacha bamb,
Aag Someshwari, bamb Rameshwari
Tithe paanyache naahin mag themb
Shing phunkeet gela paanyacha Ingreji bamb.

The British fire-engine runs screaming to Rameshwar
What a pity the fire is in Someshwar
Never mind there's no water in the tank
It is a British fire-engine after all

Not much has changed, except that we didn't have illnesses like chikanguniya, dengue and swine flu then.

Right in front of our chawl was Mannabhai's small farsaan shop. That was paradise for the children. Through the day, there was savoury sev, ghatia, bhajji and chivda of every kind and sort. They tasted different from the kind we made at home, and very good too. Mannabhai measured quantities according to his own sweet will. His brother Devdas minded the store. Mannabhai was stout and a bit of a shorty. Devdas was lean and tall.

Mannabhai was our Pied Piper; we would have followed him wherever he went so long as he was carrying a platter of bhajiyas or sev. He was a fixture at the Ramji Purushottam Chawl even unto the next generation.

But it was Kulkarni's bhajjis that were the craze of the chawl. Kulkarni's restaurant was a three- or four-minute walk from where we lived. Many young couples went there on Sunday evenings. The fare was tasty, healthy and seemed to have been cooked at home. The area around the eatery was rich with delicious aromas. That bouquet would have left the attars of Kanauj far behind.

Many young men would settle down at the Irani restaurant. The local 'Irani' was seen as a social institution in itself. Our saints have spoken about equality but you could see this in operation at the Irani restaurant. People from all castes, classes, communities and faiths were to be seen eating here. Here, all differences dissolved. You were only a *giraayak* here, a customer. Thus you would be identified by some peculiarity of your body or clothes. As you approached the cash counter, the waiter who had served you might call out, 'The topi for four annas' or

'The skinny guy is eight annas' or 'The pyjamas for a tea and bun-maska.'

At the cash box there was always a well-built Irani man. I never saw a frail Irani in my life. They were all fair-skinned with a ruddy tinge to their complexions. They would talk in high-pitched voices and so would the waiters. Some men would be reading quietly in the middle of it all. Some would discuss profound topics with serious faces. You could sit for as long as you wanted, no one would try to uproot you. In between, you could ask for a 'single', a cup of tea, to keep your account going. Many *giraayaks* were regulars. The owner would even have the waiters run errands for the regulars.

The two identifying marks of an Irani café were the marble-topped round tables and the mirrors. Each table would have four chairs arranged around it. They had names like Viceroy and Light of Asia and Sunrise.

They served as a landmark too. In the minds of the common people they were known as 'Irani hotels'. 'Go on a little and then on your left you'll find an Irani hotel,' one might say.

In one corner of the restaurant would be a glass-fronted cupboard, about half the height of an average person. It would have loaves of bread—pao—and cakes inside it. There would be a light bulb burning inside to keep the pao warm. Tantalising snacks like khari biscuits (butter biscuits) and naankhatais would nestle in heavy glass bottles. Every wall was covered with mirrors. There were mirrors even on the pillars in between. In red or green chalk would be inscribed warnings such as 'Do not comb'; or information, 'Today's Special: Chicken Rashida'.

I loved the plum cakes and the puddings at the Iranis but all that came later. In the morning, we'd buy kadak pao, a loaf with a crusty exterior; or jeera khari biscuits, flaky butter biscuits spiced with cumin. To eat a breakfast of jeera khari and tea was heaven. There was also aakuri, Parsi-style eggs scrambled with onions, tomatoes and coriander. I never did try the *baida ghotala*—literally 'a mess of eggs'—though. One of my great regrets.

The Irani restaurants had a significant role to play in the growth of the city. They united the many-feathered and many-voiced community into a single flock. To the creative species—the writers, the painters, the actors—they were a shelter akin to Mount Govardhan. They were a refuge from loneliness. But they are now beginning to disappear. Time marches on and takes some institutions with it. The Fort area still has some that continue to hold out. Near the Metro Talkies there is Kayani's and Merwan's continues near Grant Road Station. I could I suppose find out what an egg ghotala is. I should take my courage in my hands and make my way to one of these. My fondest wish is that these restaurants that have done so much for the city should thrive and prosper. Long may they live.

Bhuleshwar and Kalbadevi were full of Gujarati eating places with names like Arya Niwas and Thakkar Bhojanalaya. Near the Victoria Terminus station was Sabar Lodge; it is still there. Brahmins from the banks of the Sabar ran the place. The food was too sweet for my taste but the daal was very tasty. If you didn't finish everything you were served, the manager or the owner would ask you, full of concern: 'Why haven't you finished it all? Didn't you like it? What's wrong with it?' All the Gujaratis who came to Mumbai on business ate here.

Diwali was a big event in our chawl's calendar. All the women of the chawl would get together to make the faraal, the sweets and savouries that would be eaten and served through the season. First though, the houses had to be cleaned. Aai was passionate about cleanliness. There were no stainless steel dabbas in those days. That was all to the good. Once stainless steel invaded the kitchens, the food lost its savour. In our day, we used vessels made of copper or brass. Every week, Aai would scrub them with tamarind. She would make a hillock of them at the tap in the front. And in the middle of it would be Kashi and me. Diwali brought out the worst of her cleaning demons. She would be wiping and washing and sweeping and dusting all over the place. The vessels would grow warm with the intensity of her scrubbing. And then, perhaps mistaking us for vessels, we would be scrubbed down as well.

Nagappa would come to our home to make Diwali *faraal*. He was a Telangi cook, his skin burnt black. He wore a lungi and a loose half-sleeved shirt and had a large and capable towel over his shoulder. It so happened that Nagappa's younger sister-in-law had delivered at Dr Saibai's Ranade's maternity home. It had been a difficult delivery but Aai had handled it all perfectly. That was where Nagappa had met her and from that year on, he had begun to come to us to make our *faraal*. He brought with him a huge kadhaai, a perforated spoon and a plate with a raised rim among many other utensils and when he arrived, Ramji Purushottam Chawl knew that Diwali was near. Once he was done with us, he would be off to the Sonpatkis. Nandu would be delighted; now he was sure he would get his 'laavyaacha laalu' as he called rawa laddoos. As soon as Nagappa walked into our home, he would take off his shirt and hang it on a nail. Then he'd issue a command: 'Kaashé, make us a cawphee'. Once the cawphee was drunk, a beedi would be lit and for the next three or four hours, the delicious aromas of roasting besan or rawa would wander around the house, hanging on to the coat-tails of the acrid beedi smoke. The month of Shraavan would see my mother in full form. She would wear her sovla—a silk sari that signified purity and meant no one could touch her—and cook while wearing it. Then Babu would take some of the food for the cow in the temple. The next morsel would be for the crows. And then we could fall to.

During Shravan, Aai would read the Bhagwat, stories from the Puranas. Saturdays and Mondays were days of fasting. We only ate once on those days. In the morning, we would have to make do with sabudana khichdi. Jeera biscuits, buttered bread and other such Western food was forbidden. We had to eat before sunset on banana leaves. In the night, a fruit would have to suffice.

'You don't have to stuff your face all the time,' Aai would say. 'Good to give your tummy a rest from time to time.' To which one wanted to say, '*Aadhi Potoba, Mag Vitthoba*' or 'God be praised but first my belly be raised.' But what if she were to hear?

At that time Mumbai was full of flowers. Shravan was a particularly rich time. You could get mogra, batmogra, saayli, bakul, sonchaafa, hirwa chaafa and circlets of madanbana and saayli to put in your hair. The best places were Thakurdwar, Khetwadi, Benham Hall and Central Cinema. You could get a pudi of flowers for one anna, and a nice fat one it would be too. For two annas, you got a garland. Ganesh Chaturti turned every home into a festival of flowers. In front of every house, in the courtyard of the chawl, was a tulsi plant. Festivals were public affairs, celebrated by everyone. But there was nothing commercial about them. Every chawl had its own Ganpati. Everyone made a contribution and the whole thing was managed on what was collected. The young men of each chawl would collect from that chawl. Outsiders could not interfere. People gave what they wanted to, voluntarily. In many places, all the residents would get together and decide what they thought was a fair contribution—say, five rupees per house. Eight or ten days after the immersion, a public meeting would be called and the accounts would be made public. When some money was left over, and it often was, then a special function called an 'Alpopahar' was organised. The organisers would be thanked, the children given small gifts and tea would be served and snacks eaten. One of the respectable personages of the chawl would be appointed the president of the Ganesh Mandal. For the ten days of the festival, the president would be treated with the respect due to a viceroy. In his inaugural address, the president was supposed to begin with a reference or two to the state of the nation and the pressing questions that were facing it and then move on swiftly to the problems and concerns of the chawl. Along with the snacks and suchlike, we would get coffee spiked with elaichi. At Ramji Purushottam Chawl, there was a man called Date who brought the milk every morning. It was important to tell him: 'We'll need more milk today, Date.' All the women of the chawl got together to cook for the festival.

Since money was not important, the festival was free of commercial taint. There was no scurrying about for sponsorships. All the chawls consciously tried to keep things simple so there was no question of competitions or a competitive spirit. Since the entire festival had to be run on what was collected, no one splashed money about. There was no talk about how many crores had been spent on the deity's ornaments and no desire to build Ganesh images that were bigger than houses. For us, Ganpati coming home was a matter of joy and not an occasion for ostentation. The Janmashtami festival's pot of curds was also tied at a reasonable height. Four or five layers of the human pyramid sufficed to reach it. No one thought to tie it ten or twelve layers above the ground or to add a prize of twenty lakh rupees to the pot. There was no such excess.

It was the house helps, the Kunbis or Balyas, who formed the Govinda mandals. They would dance and that was also quite wonderful. One of their songs went as follows:

Gomu chal ga
Chowpatty bandar-la
Titha ubha aahe ga
Gokulcha Kaanha

Gomu, let's get going
To Chowpatty we will go
There Krishna of Gokul
Is standing on the shore

The Krishna of Gokul would indeed be waiting there. A young man would be dressed as Krishna and the rest of the Balyas would make him do as they pleased. He had to do their bidding.

The area where we lived was full of streets and lanes with evocative names: Ambewadi (Mango wadi), Fanaswadi (Jackfruit wadi), Tadwadi (Palm wadi), Pophalwadi (Betelnut), Kandewadi (Onion), Jambhulwadi (Java plum), Moogbhaat (Mung), Borbhaat (Berries), Kelewadi (Banana) and other fruits and vegetables right up to Amrutwadi (the Wadi of Nectar), if you please. Some wadis were named after certain people. Hemrajwadi, Dhaswadi, Khotachiwadi, Maanglaaye Kolyachiwadi (aka Mangalwadi), Gangaram Khatryachiwadi, Navalkar Lane, Bhai Jeevanji Lane. There was also a Dr Viegas Street, which is still there. Other places in our area were anointed by Gods: Kalbadevi, Babulnath, Mumbadevi, Mahalakshmi. In the Mohammed Ali road area, there was Dimtimkar Marg. There was a Tawa Street in Mohammed Ali Road. In Girgaon, there were two Gaiwadis, named for cows. In the Muslim area, there was a Bakri Adda, named for the goat. And of course, there was Kala Ghoda or the Black Horse Square.

Some important streets carried the names of English dignitaries. For instance there was Forjett Street in the Tardeo area; some names that have survived include Lamington Road, Delisle Road and Grant Road. On the Harbour Line of the Central Railway, some of the stations were Currey Road and Reay Road. On the Western Railway, the Parel station is now called Elphinstone Road. Many of these Englishmen had a deep and life-long connection with the city and Mumbaikars knew this at some level. Those who did not do much had to make to do with being memorialised in by-lanes. The Mahanagar Municipality is rather strange.

In the Lalbaug or Parel areas, chawls had names like Patra (asbestos) or Cement. They were workmanlike names which perhaps reflected the nature of the people who lived there. There is even a Dagdi Chawl near Delisle Road and everyone knows about that one.[2] Ahmed Sailor Building, Mawawala Chawl, Khandke Building, Dalvi Building, were all part of Mumbai's history and at one time were landmarks. Talmakiwadi near Tardeo was a Gaud Saraswat area. Similarly there was a Kudaldeshkarwadi in Girgaon. Right next to it was Khotachiwadi. Both these were remarkably quiet and beautiful places. Just a little beyond Opera House was Haji Kasim Wadi. Mama Warerkar lived there.

Many weekly magazines were produced in Khatauwadi in Girgaon. Khetwadi was thus a huge patchwork. Each wadi has its own character and together they faced the city. Inside, of course, it was a real labyrinth.

The Gujaratis are amongst the oldest residents of the city—from Opera House right up to Chira Bazaar. Thakurdwar, Khetwadi, C P Tank, Bhuleshwar were areas in which Gujaratis and Marathis lived in harmony. It was in the mills owned by the rich Gujaratis that poor Maharashtrians from the Konkan Coast came to make their living. In the tall buildings erected by the Gujarati traders, Marathi women worked as domestic servants. They also brought up several generations of the Gujarati seths' children. They were known as bais and were treated with great respect in the large households in which they

---

[2]Dagdi Chawl is where the gang-leader-turned politician Arun Gawli lives.

served. Young Marathi boys also worked at these homes. The Gujaratis called them Ramas.

The Gujaratis who lived in the chawl had their own businesses or they sold cloth or steel. If not, they would be employed by some businessman as accountants or in some administrative position. Thackersey and Morarjee were old wealthy business families. We had no reason to come into contact with any of them. For us the Gujaratis were represented by the grocer from Kutch. Our relationship with him was a bit stormy, to say the least. At least, on our side.

He would greet our complaints—his measures were wrong, that the rice had far too many stones in it or that the jaggery was getting watery—with the same smiling face. Then Babubhai would say in his mixture of Marathi and Gujarati, '*Biji vaar asa naai honaar*'—Next time (in Gujarati), it won't happen (in Marathi)—with great remorse. The residents of the chawl would argue that they wanted value for their money. So the goods sold should have no flaws. Babubhai would laugh and light another beedi and say, placatingly: '*Samjoochoo ben. Mee samajte. Samda samajte.*' (I understand sister—in Gujarati; I understand what you're saying—in Marathi; I understand everything—in a mixture of Marathi and Gujarati).

Gujarati homes were always extremely clean but the passages and staircases were always filthy. This did not seem to bother the Gujaratis at all. Inside their houses, they preferred blue or yellow paint. On the doors, there would be glass bead torans. On the beds, piles of mattresses and fat cushions. If you went to one of their homes, you would first be given a glass of water but you would not be allowed to leave without tea and snacks. When you were at the door, they would place mouth freshener in your hand which was a mixture of fennel and scented betelnut or some mixture like that. Right up to the door, you would be escorted with your host still talking until they said farewell. This was the traditional, *Aao-jo*, which means 'Come again, soon'.

At Navratri the Gujaratis celebrated the fertility of the earth with garba raas. Sikkanagar was close by. This was a society of well-to-do Gujaratis. We would go there to watch the garba. Khetwadi also had its garba raas, danced in the gallis and bylanes. This was a simple garba. Ten or twelve women would form a circle and dance around a beautifully decorated clay pot with a light burning inside it.

This was a symbol of fertility and creativity. I remember some of the lines of a song that was sung then.

Tame ek vaar ja jore ho Marwada
Tame Marwadni mehndi re ho Marwada
Tame oloon laavjo, peloon lavjo
Paan supari, paan-na beeda, elchi daana
Hon ke peloon lavjo re ho Marwada
Tame ek vaar ja jo re ho Marwada
Tame chitalni chundhadi lavjo re ho Marwada
Tame oloon laavjo, peloon lavjo
Paan supari, paan-na beeda, elchi daana
Hon ke peloon laavjo re ho Marwada
Tame ek vaar ja jo re ho Marwada

Just this once, when you go, Marwada
Bring me mehndi
Bring me this, bring me that

Bring me paan-supari, the ingredients such as elaichi
Use your head and bring me things to please me
Just this once, when you go Marwada
Bring me a shawl from Chital
Bring me this, bring me that
Bring me paan-supari, the ingredients such as elaichi
Use your head and bring me things to please me
Just this once when you go, Marwada

Another song:

Khamma maara Nandjina laal, morli kyaan re vaagadi?
Gopiyo dodi dodi jaaye, morli kyaan re vaagadi?
Hoon to sutiti maara shayanbhuvanma
Saambhlya morlino saad, morli kyaan re vaagadi?
Khamma mara Nandjina laal, morli kyaan re vaagadi?

Son of Nanda, where do you play that flute?
It brings the gopis running, where do you play that flute?
I was sleeping in my bedroom when
I heard the music, where do you play that flute?
Son of Nanda, where do you play that flute?

A gopika tells Krishna that his flute has driven her mad. She has no thought now for the world, no control over herself. She is in a state of love madness in which she does not care about her home or society or the world. When she sits down to churn the cream, the cat steals the butter. When she is grinding the grain, the dogs play havoc with the flour but all her attention, she says, is fixed on his flute. She asks him where he is playing it. Her little son weeps in his cradle and after all this, when she goes to sleep in her bedroom, the sound of the flute pursues her there. She asks what she is to do. This poem is by the famous Gujarati poet-saint Narsinh Mehta of the nineteenth century but it is still popular.

The Gujaratis rule the city of Mumbai to this day. There's a simple reason for this: money. The Gujaratis have a saying that has a great deal of significance for them. *Nana hoy to Nathulal, nana vagar Naththu.* (When you have money, you're Nathulal; when you don't, you're plain old Naththu). During the British Raj, there were wooden benches in the railway stations. On some were written in Gujarati script: *Fakt baanoo-on maate* (For women only). Some may still be around to this day.

Parsi and Gujarati traders have lined the streets with gold. They adjusted to local Marathi traditions. Mumbai's nature is never to accept defeat. This was the attitude that they absorbed. The Parsis had a lasting effect on the Pathare-Prabhu community. And Gujarati habits such as kite-flying were adapted joyfully into Mumbai's life. The call 'Kai po chhe' still resounds in its backlanes and derives from the Marathi shout of exultation: '*Kaaplaach aahe*' (It's truly cut) when a kite has been brought down by another.

Seventy or eighty years ago, the Parsis and Gujaratis weren't just rich; they made good use of their money. They started schools and colleges and their own social institutions. Many of the great classical singers who came out of Goa were given assistance by the Bhatias and the Kapols. They achieved much in the arenas of cinema and the stage. They were prime movers in the political sphere and even while they did all this, they tried to take the Marathi people with them. They knew that Marathis were easy to anger, that their manners were somewhat rough and ready but they were also hard-working and honest; or so the Gujaratis discovered.

As time went on things changed. The Parsis spun their own cocoons and retreated into them. The relationship between the Gujaratis and Marathis soured over the question of language and the question of Mumbai. But all this began after 1950. In our time, there were no such differences. Our common enemy was the British. There was no question about who owned the city. It belonged to all those who lived in it. In our time—and it did matter what language you spoke—everyone had feelings of gratitude and affection for the city.

Mumbai was seen as a place that could use the work of your hands and in return, it would fill your belly. Everyone was welcome, or so we thought. It was a workers' town. It only became known as a city of the rich after 1960. Earlier, it was a city of the working class. People were ready to adjust and live in peace and harmony for they felt they belonged. And after that, the next fifty years have been a period of loot and plunder. This we owe to our leaders. There has been no end to their greed. Everyone was trying to squeeze whatever profit they could out of the city.

We were followers of Gandhiji. We still owe some allegiance to him even today. He was a big man who had the interests of the nation at heart. He had an ethical influence on the country and so the local leaders, at the grassroots level, also behaved themselves and were disciplined. There was a Gandhian who lived in our area too. His speech and behaviour were gentle. He was known to keep fasts and lived an austere life. He came to be called The Girgaon Gandhi.

In truth, it was not as if the Independence Struggle had much effect on us. We did not rise every morning with the demand for independence on our lips. At one level, this was because of Mumbai's philosophy: we're fine so long as our work's fine. You got up and you went about your business. That's how the city was. Nor did the British get in our way much. Their administrative systems were near-perfect. Most inhabitants of our chawl were followers of Lokmanya Tilak so we had no idea what Gandhiji was up to most of the time. People around us would say that you could not tell when he would change his course, when he would modify his stance. After 1940, this began to change. And by 1942, the struggle for independence had become an angry, vocal one.

Let me share a memory from my childhood. I must have been about three or four years old when I began to hear the English words, 'Go back, Simon' from time to time. When we were playing and had a fight one of us might say to the other, 'Go back, Simon!' Our mother also talked about this. 'Nowadays people are really angry with the British. How much of this "Go back, Simon" is going on.' It was only many years later that I learned that seven members of the British parliament had been sent under Sir John Simon to talk to the leaders of the Independence movement. Various demonstrations had been organised and people waved a lot of black flags at him. There were processions and meetings all over the city, all echoing the cry, 'Simon, go back'. Simon must have gone home, empty-handed, unaware that his name was still floating around the Ramji Purushottam Chawl.

The political atmosphere began to heat up after 1940. We were feeling the pinch of the Second World War. Rationing had been imposed on us. There was a shortage of grain and that awful Brazilian rice had the consistency of sago. There was no kerosene for the stoves. Life became difficult and every day brought fresh horror stories.

Anna Chaudhury, our neighbour, would keep Aai abreast of the developments after he had read his paper. 'Have you heard, Babi's Mum? Hitler seems to be set on marching to Moscow.' Aai would drag herself to Princess Street and back, carrying the burden of this news, always worried about what would happen to us. If a bomb were to fall on our chawl, Nanda's mother would naturally look out for Nandu and Bhavdya. But who would be around to look after her three? It became difficult for her to go to work. Then there was talk about evacuating Mumbai. Nanda and family would head back to Pune. The Chaudhuris would take Dayanath off to the village. A knot of fear would form in her stomach as she wondered what would become of us. When she had the night shift, the three of us would huddle together and somehow get through the night. Messrs Hitler and Co had us all shook up.

You would not believe how cheap Mumbai was before the war. Onions? Two annas a rattal[3]. Potatoes were three. A coconut was three paise; an anna for a good fat one. Kerosene cost seven paise a big bottle. Mutton was nine annas a rattal. A vaata[4] of prawns was eight annas. And a pair of pomfret? Three and a half rupees. If you went to the docks and bought fish, it was even cheaper.

---

[3]A rattal was about half a kilo. The gazetteer for Akola puts a rattal at 39 tolas. A tola is 11.66 grams. So a rattal is about 454.74 grammes by my understanding.

[4]A vaata is a portion. Fisherwomen arrange the prawns in circular mounds.

As for cloth, a rather flashy georgette sari was fourteen to fifteen rupees. The cloth was of excellent quality. It would not tear on washing. And if it turned out bad, you didn't have to fight with the shopkeeper to get it replaced. An ordinary sari cost two rupees, at the most three. A pair of chappals cost one-and-a-half to two-and-a-half rupees and they were good sturdy things too. You bought a pair and you didn't bother about another for the next two years.

Tickets to the cinema? Four annas for the pit. Above that were the eight-anna seats, twelve annas[5], and two-and-a-half rupees for the box. A good strong cup of tea that could make a corpse get up and walk cost one anna. You could get a blouse stitched for four annas and milk was four annas a seer[6]. My mother would say that when she got married, gold was twenty rupees a tola and we found that difficult to believe. But then when I got married in 1947, gold was seventy rupees a tola and people find that difficult to believe now.

Mumbai was truly a heavenly city. We are told that Paradise has trees laden with salted almonds and shelled pistachio, that the hills have rivers of milk running down them. Mumbai was like that.

So how do I remember the price of onions after so many years, my neighbours and friends ask me. What harm is there in remembering good things? Today—as

---

[5]The rupee had sixteen annas. Thus 'four annas' is the equivalent of twenty-five paise, eight annas is fifty paise and twelve annas is seventy-five paise. The rupee went metric in 1957 but the usage continued in daily life and in Bollywood songs: '*Paanch rupaiyya baarah aana*' from *Chalti ka Naam Gaadi* (Satyen Bose, 1958).

[6]One seer is the equivalent of 1.024 litres or one litre, really.

I write this—onions are seventy-five to eighty rupees a kilo. Should I remember this terrible thing? Is this what I should recount to the next generation? That onions cost seventy-five rupees a kilo in this city?

At another level, people say they are willing to accept that onions might have been two paise a rattal but they also add that people's salaries were also correspondingly low. I can tell you about our family. Aai's salary was sixty rupees a month and we managed very well on that. We were happy. Today young people earn sixty to seventy thousand a month—at least the educated ones do. And yet they complain and whine. It might be that these handsome salaries are spent on the cost of the good life, entertainment, clothes, children's education, those endless classes and tuitions, the dinners out or something, I don't know. Be that as it may, what I wanted to say was simply this: the Second World War gave Mumbai its first taste of high prices. They say this war changed the course of world history and rewrote its geography too. And at this time too, something changed the lives of the residents of Ramji Purushottam Chawl. And because of that I ended up in the world of theatre.

Let me tell you about that.

*

I don't remember the exact date. I don't even remember the year. I was about thirteen or fourteen then. Aai was on night duty. Kashi was in Pune on training. Only Babu and I were at home. It was around midnight. The entire chawl was asleep. So were Babu and I. And then a knock on the door, a thunderous knock. Babu woke up first and roused me. Then he opened the door. Outside: two policemen.

'Laxmibai Lotlikar lives here right?' one asked in a stern voice. No one had ever spoken her name in such dry bureaucratic accents before. Both Babu and I could hardly get a word out.

'Acid has fallen on her body. You'll have to come with us to the hospital,' the other constable said in a slightly kinder voice. Babu and I burst into tears.

We went to the Chaudhurys and told them what had happened. Slowly, the residents of the chawl got to know and came to our door. Acid? On your Aai? How? What happened? Which parts are affected?

The police had no details. 'Come to the hospital,' they said.

Babu and I went. Chaudhury Tai and Nanda's Aai came with us. The police went ahead in a jeep. We took a taxi and followed them to Gokuldas Tejpal Hospital, near Victoria Terminus. I had always been in awe of taxis. This was the first time I had been in one. But what a terrible way to achieve a dream.

Aai was in the general ward. She was lying on her face. She was wearing a sari beneath the waist and above that we could not see because she was covered with a net. There was no way to tell anything else.

'Babu, how did you get here?' she managed to ask when she realised that we were there. And then she began to groan and asked for some water.

Next to her cot a water container had been placed. In her mouth a pipe had been fixed. She had to suck the water slowly. Her hair, which was long and thick, had been tied to the cot so that it would not fall on her back and stick there. She was lying on her stomach.

I looked at her and I was filled with horror. How had this happened to my firm and resolute Aai? Now, when I think back to the time, I strongly feel that Destiny treats us like toys. We are like puppets, at the receiving end of her whims and fancies.

The police had taken down her statement. She had no idea what had happened or how. She had been climbing the steps at Dr Saibai Ranade's clinic when she suddenly became aware that something hot and burning had fallen on her back, as if needles of fire were running into her. She fell down the stairs, writhing in agony.

Aai's attitude to life had always been to keep herself to herself. She did her work well and did not like anyone doing her favours. She had no enemies, nor did she get too friendly with anyone. Aai was asked if she felt someone had done this deliberately, with malice aforethought. Her answer was, 'No'. The police at the Princess Street Police Station had registered the case as an accident.

I still have some unanswered questions about what happened that night. I find it difficult to believe that she was climbing the stairs of Dr Saibai's Hospital and acid should have just happened to splash all over her. It seemed to me, then as now, that someone had done this deliberately. There was no reason for there to be bottles of acid lying around the stairs. And even if we were to accept, for the purposes of argument, that a bottle just 'happened' to be on the stairs, how did it 'happen' to splash itself on my mother? It seemed that this might be part of a well thought-out plan.

Who did it, then? Every workplace has its share of conflicts. Workers will often find themselves at loggerheads. But none of this seemed to have happened at Dr Saibai's hospital. It was a small place anyway. Aai handled almost everything there. There were one or two young men but the rest of the staff was female. There was no reason for the cleaners or cooks or sweepers to hate Aai.

There was one major possibility, though. Aai was young and beautiful. She was also a widow and a nurse. Had someone looked at her with lust in his eyes? And had he thrown acid at her when she had rejected him? Was this why she had been subjected to this monstrous attack? And had she done this to protect us? These thoughts would go round and round in my head until it was numb. And fire would fill me from head to foot.

Society did not look upon nurses with a sympathetic eye. Nursing is a profession dedicated to caring and healing. But this is the positive way of looking at it. Our society is a hypocritical one. It repeats these things parrot-fashion. It does not act according to what it says. Nurses are called 'Sister' but in reality, they are seen as women who clean the shit and piss of patients. And widows are no higher in this terrible social hierarchy. A widow is seen as fair game, she is supposed to be available to every man who wants her. Aai was both nurse and widow. Was the acid attack part of this way of seeing widows and nurses?

We brought Aai home in a taxi at midnight after three months in the hospital. Her diet was restricted. She was to eat simple food. No spices, no sour foods, nothing oily. And a whole slew of pills. There were two or three creams that had to be used on her back. We had to leave her back uncovered for as long as possible. She had to lie on her stomach.

At dawn, at five a.m. or thereabouts, I had to take her to the 'back tap' with a thin cloth over her back. Then she had to be sponged down. The cooking was taken over entirely by Nanda's Mum and Chaudhury Tai. Nanda's Mum cooked for Aai. Babu and I ate at Chaudhury Tai's. For three or four months, these families took care of us without any thought of recompense, with no expectations. To have such neighbours can only be counted as a blessing.

I now remember only the vague outlines of a story from the *Mahabharat*. It is, however, the kind of story whose essence you do not forget once you have heard it. At the end of the war, Lord Krishna takes his leave of the Pandavas. 'Ask for any boon you want,' he says. 'and it will be yours.' Kunti's turn comes first. 'Lord, I don't want much but from time to time send us some misery, some pain,' she says. Lord Krishna is a bit taken aback.'Why ask for that? Ask for something good.' Kunti laughs with a touch of sadness. 'When you're happy the mind becomes lazy. In pain, we tend to turn to God.'

This is what happened to Aai. Her devotion to God became much stronger. Once, she said to me, 'Babi, look at God's mercy. What if the acid had fallen on my face? I would have been permanently handicapped. I might even have gone blind. What would we have done then? Good it fell on my back.'

She had always had a good relationship with God. She felt you had to access the 'godhead' with all you had.

But she was not superstitious. She did not believe in 'godmen'.

'If a godman has too many demands, the gods also forsake you,' she would say. She believed that people should achieve their intended aims by sincere hard work because God also assists such endeavours. She felt that there is no need to make deals with God—you should ask Him for a clear conscience, the rest is up to you. Education, she believed, would help you make the best of yourself. If you could not study for some reason, you should acquire a skill or a craft.

However, I had to end my education after the acid attack. Aai felt terrible about this but there was no help for it. Babu could not be asked to leave school and sit at home. He was in the matriculation year. Once he cleared that, he could get a job and help with the household. Kashi was still training as a nurse. Who was to look after Aai? She needed a lot of care. She had to be helped to do everything. And so, driven to the wall, Aai agreed to let me leave school. She grieved over this. She often said, 'I felt so bad that Babi could not study.'

One had to send a request in those days to be removed from the rolls of the school. Bodhebai understood. She called me to her office and made thorough inquiries into our household affairs. One day, she even came home and sat with Aai for ten to fifteen minutes. As she was leaving she said, 'Face this with courage. You are intelligent. Do not lose hope. If you need any help, do not hesitate to ask me.'

I was unhappy about leaving school. I still regret it. My dream was to be a doctor like Dr Saibai Ranade, who was my ideal in those days. In those days there was also a famous Dr Jhirad[7]. I got to read about Dr Anandibai Joshi and was very moved by her devotion to her work. Dr Shantabai Saptarishi was also a well-known name then. I wanted to go abroad and earn the highest degrees possible in medicine. I believe that healing the sick is one of the greatest humanitarian services you can render unto others. In curing a disaease, the doctor gives his patient a new lease of life. When I was acting, I once confided this thwarted ambition to the celebrated playwright Mama Warerkar. I said, 'I wanted to be a doctor. Doctors wield such extraordinary power.' He replied, 'Listen Babi, in some ways an actor is like a doctor. If a doctor cures by using pills and potions or performing an operation, a playwright or an actor cures with different tools. We take care of society. When the audience watches a great play with fine performances, their fatigue slowly dissipates. With a calm and clear mind, the audience goes home. Their anger and negativity has been banished. That is a form of nurturance, wouldn't you say?'

I understood what he was trying to say. Great art has powers of healing. A great film or a great play can purge the mind of workaday cares and leave you elevated. That is the power of art.

*

It took a year or a year-and-a-half for Aai to recover. She began to move about the house. She was left with a white

---

[7]This refers to Dr Jerusha J. Jhirad. For those interested Abigail Jhirad wrote a book about her: *A Dream Realised: A Biography of Dr Jerusha J Jhirad* (ORT India). She was known as Jhiradbai.

scar the size of a thali. Babu would help me with the cooking. I would do what she told me to and so I learned cooking under her guidance.

Aai had, of course, lost her job. Dr Saibai Ranande did come over once or twice to ask after Aai's health. 'If you need anything, you have only to tell me,' she said with great warmth. 'Don't feel shy.' Aai's eyes filled with tears; Dr Saibai's were wet too.

Here is a memory of Dr Saibai. One day, her cook quit suddenly. Aai was working at the clinic. She told Dr Saibai, 'Until you find a new cook, I'll cook for you if you don't object.' Dr Saibai said immediately, 'I don't place any importance in these things. I'd be happy to have you cook for me.' Aai cooked for her for a month. And Dr Saibai said to her, 'Your Babi is far too thin. Send her to me from time to time.' Dr Saibai lived above her clinic. When I went to see her, she would give me a cup of cream to eat. She started me off on Waterbury's Compound, a therapeutic vitamin tonic, and cod liver oil. Every week I would be invited to have lunch with her. Sometimes Babu would also be invited. The food was very tasty, cooked in the Brahmin style.

They say one should be able to show one's love for others. But one should also be able to accept love from others. One should be able to accept such love as comes one's way with an open heart and grace. One ought not to demand more nor ought one to wish for more. This is what my generation learned in childhood. It seems as if today this is no longer the case. People now seem suspicious of love, even if it is pure and unselfish. And yet they become ever bolder in their attempts and methods of trying to find love. One can never be fulfilled in this manner. Such has been my experience. There would probably be others who love the world, like me. Can their struggle be understood? Who can tell.

I was talking about Saibai Ranade. 'If you need anything let me know', she had said and such was her generosity of spirit, she meant it too. But could we have sent her a grocery list every month? How were we to manage, that was the question before us. Aai no longer had a salary. We were living on her savings.

Then, someone turned up—almost like a character in a play who changes everything by catalysing the lives of the others. His name was Ramchandra Varde. He was a reputed director and he had been looking for us.

Varde Master was a Saraswat; and that too from our own village. Someone had told him about the acid incident. He had come to inquire about us. He soon came to know the whole story. He then told Aai about Parshwanath Altekar's Little Theatre Group. He said, 'Lakshmibai, Altekar is trying to change the face of theatre. He has some novel ideas, some interesting dreams. He is an educated man. He's just started the Little Theatre Group to train young men and women for the theatre. Send Babi to him. She'll be paid thirty rupees a month.'

Aai did not need much persuasion. We could bump along on thirty rupees a month but it was not just the money although we certainly needed that. I admire my mother who, though uneducated, could still understand Altekar's dreams of a theatrical education.

'Babi, look on it as an education,' she said to me. 'Your schooling was left incomplete. Now at least you can study this way. If it's something you can do, if it's something you like doing, go on with it. If not, you can stop. I won't force you either way.'

Two days later, Varde Master took me to Mantri Building near Opera House. B R Deodhar's Gandharva Sangeet Mahavidyalaya was there. In the large hall, Altekar held his classes.

Varde Master presented me to Dada. (Everyone called Altekar 'Dada'.) He spared me a casual glance. Mama Warerkar was also present. He called me to him and drew me out gently. He wanted to know who I was, how many members there were in my family, why I had abandoned my education. When I said I was from Ratnagiri, he had a good laugh. He had the open-hearted laugh of a child. 'Tomorrow at eight a.m.,' Altekar said. I touched their feet and went home.

Training ran from eight a.m. to eleven. There were six or seven of us: Sunder Nayampalli who later became a star of the silent cinema and after that of the talkies as well; his wife Kalyani, Vasant Gawankar, Kavi Raja Badhe, his friend Bakul, Ramchandra Varde and I. Later many other students joined us. Everyone had a soft spot for me, perhaps because I was the youngest.

Altekar was a good-looking man. He was dark but had fine features. He was well-built and had an impressive personality. He generally wore trousers and a bush-shirt. From time to time, he would exchange this for a dhotar and coat. He had large shining eyes, a high forehead, his hair slicked back. He always seemed to have an intense, enigmatic look on his face. He wanted to infuse fresh ideas into theatre.

Sangeet Natak as a form was beginning to seem old and tired even to its loyal audiences. Those five-to-six hour extravaganzas seemed boring and baggy. Jowly men playing women's roles were also becoming unacceptable. Times were changing and cinema was accelerating those changes. It was felt that plays should be short and meaningful and tightly scripted.

Or so the new ideas went. And in this movement were educated writer-actors such as Anant Kanekar, Nandu Khote, Keshavrao Date, K Narayan Kale and Parshwanath Altekar. But its leader, its sutradhar, was Mama Warerkar.

With the revolutionary idea that women should play women's roles on the stage, Parshwanath Altekar, Nandu Khote and Sundar Nayampalli started an independent company called Radio Stars in 1931 and presented its first play, *Baby*. Later, this company brought plays like *Paanchali*, *Swastik Bank* and Prabhodankar Thackeray's *Khara Brahmin* (The Real Brahmin), all tightly scripted, two-hour performances to the stage. But the most successful was Anant Kanekar's *Aandlyaachi shaala* (School of the Blind). This was presented by Natyamanvantar and starred Keshavrao Date and Jyotsnabai Bhole in the lead roles. Jyotsnabai was asked to sing some songs too. It was based on a European play, *A Gauntlet* by the Norwegian playwright Björnstjerne Björnson, who won the Nobel Prize for Literature in 1903. It was an experimental production with which Marathi cinema truly came of age. That we now have experimental and meaningful theatre owes much to ground-breaking plays like *Baby*, *Aandhalyaacha shaala* and *Panchaali*.

Credit should go to Anant Kanekar, K Narayan Kale,

Sundar Nayampalli, Nandu Khote, Mama Warerkar, Keshavrao Date and Parshwanath Altekar. Rangayan[8] later took these ideas forward. It is a sad truth that while Vijay Tendulkar, Vijaya Mehta and Madhav Vatve have been given the credit for experimental theatre, Altekar Dada has been ignored. This bothers me. I am not denying the significance or the contribution made by Vijayabai or Vijay Tendulkar. I am only saying that Altekar also deserved some credit.

Every day we met to study at Deodhar Mahavidyalaya in the big hall. In the middle of the hall, two tables were placed. One small table was placed crosswise. It was at this table that Altekar sat. The students sat at the big tables to listen to the lectures. He would talk about the fundamental principles of theatre. This was our theory section. What does a play mean? What are we saying in the play? If the job of the actor is to convey to the audience the words that the writer has put down, what should the actor bear in mind when doing so? The written play and the production are two completely different things. How does this happen? What does a rehearsal mean? What is the importance of the spoken word? Altekar would talk about all this to us. For the first two or three months, I didn't understand much. I couldn't even pronounce Stanislavsky. But I paid careful attention to what Altekar

---

[8]Rangayan was an experimental theatre group started by actor-director Vijaya Mehta, playwright Vijay Tendulkar, and actors Madhav Vatve and Arvind Deshpande. It had a limited number of shows for each production as it conceived of each play as an experiment and that once the experiment was conducted and replicated, the group should move on.

and Mama Warerkar said and tried to make sure that if I did not understand something, I asked.

'I cannot tell you what good acting is or how you should act. You will have to figure that out for yourself. I can only tell you what constitutes a good performance and create in you the desire to be a good actor. That is the limit of my aim,' Altekar Dada would say. And it is true. 'Acting is something you have to learn on your own. It is a solitary process. When many solitary processes come together and connect with each other, you can say that it is time to raise the curtain and ring the third bell,' he would say.

There were large photographs of the actors of yore that were supposed to correspond with the rasas: surprise, fear, anger, love…We were not supposed to make faces that corresponded to these emotions and let it go at that. They had to be felt, we were told, at some deep level in the mind and then converted into action and emotion. Surprise can be shown in a variety of ways. So can love. On stage an actor must be aware of her body language, her make-up, she must think out everything that contributes to her performance. On stage, she must be able to use her body imaginatively and economically.

Many of these things meant little to me when we were studying in that big hall but suddenly, when I was on the stage, stories he had told us or things he had said would become clear.

Altekar paid a great deal of attention to our voices. He tried to make sure that we learned breath control and made us work on our pronunciation. Mama Warerkar wrote us tongue twisters that I still remember to this day.

The entire sentence goes:

Kalakaarachya antakarnachya sakhol gartetoon nirmaan honaarya bhaavanaanchya uttung lahirieenchya khalbalataana prasaaran paavnaari jeevnaachi sooksham vichoshtiye udbhoot vhaayla kontyaachi kalavantala parkyaancha bojad bhashechi usanvaar bhalaavaani karaavi laagat naahin. (No actor should seek to steal the style of someone else's speech but she should seek within, in the sounding shoals of her heart and her self for those shores of such sentiment that are thrown up by tremors left behind by subtle experiences.)

Try it. One breath. Go on. You'll find yourself gasping at the end. I am not even sure what it means but this convoluted sentence of Warerkar has stayed with me over all these years as an unforgettable lesson in voice culture. I find it odd sometimes that I cannot remember things that happened last week but this tongue twister is with me still, even though I learned it seventy years ago. What does a vowel mean? How can a vowel be projected? How should one train one's voice for the theatre? What is the diet one should follow? How should one stress a word? How should one aim at illuminating the meaning of a sentence so that it becomes crystal clear? How does one modulate one's pitch? Altekar worked with us on all this for days on end.

I used to speak with a typically Konkan drawl. Mama Warerkar set me right on that one. 'Babi, you can't speak like that on stage. It's okay if you have to play a Konkani character but otherwise you have to learn to speak standard Marathi. Why should your audience be made aware of your being from the Konkan for no reason?'

My voice was thin and high-pitched. Altekar cured me

of this with his voice culture classes. Like a musician gets up in the early morning and practises the lower octave, so also the tongue-twisters and voice culture classes helped us develop our voices. It is important to note that Altekar was one of the first to realise how important an actor's voice was and that she should focus on it. I had only studied up to the seventh standard. The credit for my pronunciation being clear and my voice having improved in range and depth must go to Altekar.

I have already told you that our classes were held in B R Deodhar's Sangeet Vidyalaya. Deodhar had done much research on the subject of the voice but he had never, even by mistake, considered the interior landscape of the artist. 'That isn't something I can manage,' he would say. 'You keep at it.' Altekar would try and get him to think about it but Deodhar was having none of it. When he arrived to collect the rent, Altekar would sometimes mischievously suggest: 'Yes, sure, but first you must tell us about the effect of singing on an artist's mindscape.' Often Deodhar Master would simply scuttle off saying, 'Go on with what you're doing'. He would then vanish for the next two or three hours. From time to time Kumar Gandharva would also visit Deodhar Master.

Altekar was a Jain. He lived the simple life of a seeker. He neither smoked nor drank. He didn't even drink tea. He never married. If the stage or the cinema are worlds that leave most people looking like they have been in a coalpit, Altekar's reputation was spotless. It is said that when an actress tried to seduce him, he had her thrown out of the play. His principles were simple. Concentrate on what your goal is. Live simply. Sacrifice. Wear yourself out in the pursuit of your dreams.

Dada Altekar had a great devotion to Mama Warerkar. Dada took part in whatever Mama did. Mama too depended on Altekar in a variety of ways. Once or twice a month, Dada would take all of us to an Irani café called Elias near the Deodar Sangeet Vidyalaya. He never had much money. 'Everyone take out one anna. I'll pay the rest,' he would say. This one-anna rule did not apply to me, Dada made it clear right from the beginning. This was because I was the youngest. We would all eat things like brun-maska, cakes, omelettes, pastries, bread with jam and butter or khari biscuits.

Altekar lived at Khar. He had bought a small bungalow there. It even had a little theatre. Next door was Sunder Nayampalli's bungalow. Nayampalli was tall and strapping. Dada Altekar, Nayampalli, Nandu Khote, P Jairaj and Raja Sandow were the he-man stars of that time. There was a gymnasium close to Opera House where these pehelwan stars would exercise every evening. Master Bhagwan Palav and his brother Harishchandra Palav were famous wrestlers from Dadar. Master Bhagwan Palav became well known when he acted in action films. John Cavas was the action star of the Wadia Company.

At that time Sunder Nayampalli was working with Killick Nixon. He left when Altekar invited him to join the Imperial Film Company. Altekar was then a big director at Imperial. Nayampalli's sister married Nandu Khote. The famous actress Shubha Khote is Nandu Khote's daughter. Sunder Nayampalli's wife Kalyani had delivered a child at Dr Saibai Ranade's clinic. Both Sunder and Kalyani knew my mother well. When I joined Altekar's unit, I was introduced to Nayampalli. When he heard that I was Lakshmibai Lotlikar's daughter, he was delighted. He came to our house and asked my mother's permission to take me to his home for a couple of days. Kalyani was also happy to see me. Their little son, who was about two years old, was very sweet. Later they had a daughter too: Lakshmi Nayamapalli. When she grew up, she achieved no little success in the world of classical music.

When I was studying with Altekar Dada, Aai had to go back to the Konkan. Some of our money was still stuck there. She also had to sort out something to do with our inheritance. Basically, the family in Adivré had not given us our due. She had asked for her Ganpati rights[9] but they had refused that too. It was not possible for me to accompany her. 'Lakshmibai, now don't worry about a thing. We will look after Babi,' Mama Warerkar said. Aai took Babu and went. I stayed for those ten to twelve days that she was away with Mama Warerkar at his home in Haji Kasim Wadi in a three-storeyed building. Mama lived on the ground floor in a spacious room. There were three of them: Mama, his sister who had been widowed young and the cook, another young widow. Mama would joke, 'Three widows live here,' he would say pointing at his bald head, referring to the tradition by which widows had their heads shaved. He was a small-made man; he could fit into your fist. He would wear a dhotar and kurta and the large round spectacles that were common at the time. Behind those spectacles, his eyes sparkled with mischief. He always had a bidi tucked between the last two fingers

[9]When a family starts Ganpati pooja, it must be continued, even after the death of the householder. Lakshmibai Lotlikar must have thought she had the right to continue the Ganpati pooja started at Adivré.

of his right hand. 'I am a playwright. I write plays about the working class. I'm like the chimneys of the textile mills. They spew smoke, I write plays,' he would say, half in jest. Mama needed gallons of tea to keep him going. He would sprawl in an easy chair, a cup of tea at hand, a packet of bidis in front of him and he would begin to talk.

There was a touch of Konkan cunning in his nature. He was never straightforward in his speech. He had a fund of jokes and anecdotes. The house was always filled with people coming and going, friends, relatives, neighbours. Tea was always a-bubble on the fire. Conversation flowed through that room, an unstoppable river. There were writers, publishers, directors and others associated with the film world, Mama was in the middle of it all, and loved it.

Mama had spent about twenty years of his life working in a post office in the Ratnagiri district of Malwan. That had damaged his right arm. In retirement, the pain only increased and so he got himself a secretary to take dictation. It seems as if an army of secretaries worked with Mama. When one left, another joined. The author Shantabai Shelke, H V Desai, Parshwanath Altekar, the editor of *Mouj*, Ram Patwardhan, the publisher V V Bhatt, all were at one time or another his writers. The last chapter of his autobiography, *Mazha Naatki Sansaar*[10] (My Theatrical World) has a list of the forty or forty-two people who played this role.

Mama read voraciously. In his house at Raghavwadi, he had a huge library. When I stayed with him, I learned

[10]*Maazha Naatki Sansaar* was published posthumously by Popular Prakashan.

he was mad about the radio. When everyone was asleep, he would listen to Western programmes on his own. The other thing was that he ate peanuts and jaggery every night. It wouldn't be far wrong to say that his night meal consisted of a plate of roasted peanuts. 'The heart is an engine, Babi,' he would say. 'It needs oil. Peanuts have lots of oil. Your brain gets a lot of energy from that oil too.'

At heart, Mama was a feminist. He believed that women should be educated and progress in every field. I would call him the first feminist I met. He believed that women should act in plays. The age of female impersonators was over, according to him, and theatre had to change with the times. Mama's encouragement brought a whole host of women to the stage: Sindhu Gadgil, Gulab Kenkre, Kanchanmala Shirodkar, Girijabai Kelkar. Girijabai was the famous singer and actor Jyotsnabai Bhole's elder sister.

If these women ventured on to the stage it was because of Mama and Altekar. In Mama's play *Udti paankhre* (Birds in flight), he sketched the portrait of a woman who rebels against her father. His daughter Maya Chitnis insisted she would act in it and did a very good job too. Mama was delighted.

Maya Chitnis was short and good-looking like her father. When I joined Mama's company, Mai (all of us, including Mama, called Maya-tai Mai) married the Royist[11] Dr G V Chitnis. Later, she became a producer in Akashvani Mumbai.

[11]Followers of Dr Monobendra Nath Roy, founder-member of the Communist Party of India and the Mexican Communist Party, were known as Royists. (He was also the husband of Leela Chitnis, the film actor.)

One day, when I was staying with Mama, he felt like eating mutton. He gave the cook the day off. 'Have you ever cooked mutton, Babi?' he asked. I hadn't but I knew Aai's recipe. 'Okay, let's give it a shot together,' he said.

The mutton came out well but it took a while to cook. 'Gosh,' said Mama. 'I could have written a play in that much time.'

When Mai came back that night from her marital home, Mama served her some mutton too. He was quite the foodie. He ate a limited amount but enjoyed what he ate.

I acted in Mama's play, *Saraswat*. It was my first role and the first performance happened at the Royal Opera House theatre on November 1, 1942. It was performed by the students of the National Theatre Academy. Altekar played two separate characters. Kalyani Nayampalli, Kanchanmala Shirodkar and I played the three female roles. Ramchandra Varde, Tryambak Gokhale (Reema Lagoo's maternal uncle), Shankar Oak and Vasant Gawankar played the other roles. B R Deodhar scored the music with customary skill. *Saraswat* was not a three-act play in the traditional sense. It's a combination of two stories with an internal thematic link.

My role in *Saraswat* happened quite suddenly. Actually rehearsals had already begun. Altekar had already finalized his three actresses. Whether you had a role or not was quite immaterial. If you worked with Altekar, you had to attend all the rehearsals. And so I was there every day, watching as he explained the production problems, talked about how he would handle the sets. He taught us everything, even how to do our own make-up, Dada taught us all the words we needed to know about the language of theatre, words like drop curtain, wing, entry, floodlights, prompting, glance, soliloquy, the stage whisper, expressions.

And so *Saraswat* was proceeding well in rehearsal. Mama was very happy. He would come regularly to rehearsals and watch, pulling away at his beedi. *Saraswat* was one of his most important plays, in terms of theme and technique. When only about a week was left for the first show, one of the actresses had a row with Altekar and marched off the stage, announcing that she would not work with him. Everyone was shocked. The big question was what would happen to the play. They had already begun running advertisements. Dada came and asked me, 'Do you know the lines?' I said I did. After all, I had been at every one of the rehearsals. Naturally, I had learned the lines by heart and additionally, Mama Warerkar wrote in a simple, lucid style.

'Come on, stand up with me,' Altekar said. He ran me through my lines a couple of times. I only appeared in the first act. After that, Dada spoke to Balakrishna Raje and Ramchandra Varde. 'Take Babi to Maganlal Dresswalla[12]. Tell him she has to be turned into a thirty-five-year-old woman.' Raje was in charge of sets and production.

At Maganlal Dresswalla, I was measured for my costume. I had to be padded up and a pair of glasses set upon my nose. Dada said, 'Be careful when you are on

[12]Near-legendary costumier, Maganlal Dresswalla was started by Harilal Dresswalla in 1926 and after his death, the business was carried on by his brother Maganlal. Initially, they did costumes for Ram Leela performances but soon branched out into films and theatre.

stage. Those glasses don't have lenses. If you put your fingers through them, people will laugh.'

Saraswat ran to a full house. The audience loved it. Both Altekar and Warerkar were pleased with my performance. After the curtains had come down, the actor Keshavrao Date came backstage to say that the role of Sumitra had been performed very well. He wanted to know who the actress was. I had changed out of my costume and was presented to him in my parkar and polka, my usual clothes. Date was astounded, '*Aaho*, who is this slip of a girl who can play Altekar's wife on stage?' Mama was delighted. A case had been filed against *Udti paankhre*. It was claimed that he had defamed Gopal Krishna Gokhale in the play. This had upset him so he was happy with *Saraswat*'s success. It was also a big thing that the first show had been at the Opera House, at that time, an extremely prestigious location. Prithviraj Kapoor had presented *Deewaar* and *Pathan* on that very stage. M G Rangnekar had staged *Aashirwad* (Blessings) and *Kul-vadhu* (Daughter-in-law of a Respectable Family) there. Altekar and Rangnekar had had a mighty dust-up over the theatre. In order to prevent Altekar from showing there, Rangnekar had booked every Saturday and Sunday for three months. Altekar had repaid him in time using the same tactics. This is where he had mounted *Saraswat*.

Aai and Babu came to see the show. Both of them liked it very much. They also liked my acting. Everyone in the chawl had heard about it. After the show, the neighbours gathered around to congratulate me. As I went to sleep that night, scenes from the past ten to twelve years began to pass before my sleepy eyes, as if I were watching a film.

Adivré, Aai bringing us back from there, the trip by sea, Aai's wet eyes, her nursing training, my school, Dr Saibai Ranade, our teacher Godhebai. All those scenes were acted out in the theatre of my mind. This is one play that does not appear before the audience. One sees it alone, in the dark.

On the Gujarati Stage

Dada Altekar taught us everything we knew. He worked us hard as actors but then every director does this. Vijayabai Mehta, for instance, would take workshops for actors for ten to twelve years. Rangnekar, Master Dattaram, Damu Kenkre, Purushottam Darvekar, are some of the directors who have scrubbed and polished dozens of actors for the Marathi stage.

Dada even taught us how to do our own make-up. There was a large department store in Ballard Estate, called Whiteway & Laidlaw, if memory still serves me right. On Dada's instructions, I went there and bought myself a tin of Max Factor. I was instructed to mix tube 27 and tube 29 in equal parts and apply this to my face.

Once, a young woman came to the Little Theatre School. She said she wanted to learn acting. She had done a fine job of her own make-up. She had even painted her nails which were long and well-kept.

'What have you done to yourself?' Dada asked this woman in a harsh voice.

'I want to act,' she said hesitantly.

'Sure, why not?' he replied. 'But why so much make-up? You might need it on the stage but you're not on the stage right now, are you? Do you see doctors wandering about with their syringes and their thermometers outside their clinics?'

'But I like using make-up, Dada,' she said plaintively.

'Then learn how to use it properly. You've smeared it all over your face,' he said. 'And anyway, learning make-up is in the distant future. First you have to learn the rudiments of stagecraft.'

The woman did join the school but she did not last very long.

Many years later, I met her again. She was now the mother of two and had grown nice and round. But still she had drawn vivid patterns of colour all over her face. 'What can I do?' she sighed, a bit shame-faced. 'I like make-up. I can't break the habit now.' When there was a production on, I would use make-up. But otherwise, I would not use even face powder. As soon as the play was done, I would clear the make-up off using oil and scrub my face clean and join the crowds going home.

*

In 1944, Marathi theatre completed a hundred years and a huge theatre festival was organized in Sangli by the Mumbai Marathi Sahitya Sangh. Mama Warerkar and Dr A N Bhalerao of the MMSS took the lead in getting it together. In February, there was also a large festival at Mumbai. The playground at the Robert Money High School in Grant Road would play host to a week of plays, a different one each day. Pendharkar put on *Satteche Ghulam*, Rangnekar's Natya Niketan presented *Kanyadan*. On that very day Kasturba Gandhi died and the show was cancelled. The festival also featured *Saraswat* and Acharya Atre's *Udyacha sansar* (The world of tomorrow). Both plays were much appreciated.

After two months, Dr Bhalerao decided to organize a grand festival of theatre. As a great aficionado of theatre it was not inconceivable for him to take charge of such a huge event and to spend so much money on it. Dr Bhalerao had a large stage erected on the sands of Chowpatty. Arrangements were made for four to five thousand people to watch the plays. *Saraswat* was also chosen as one of the plays. The production went well and the audience was enthusiastic. As children we had sometimes come to the beach with Aai and played with shells. Acting there now in *Saraswat* I thought about those shell playthings. Actors in some ways are also like playthings or dolls.

*

The Mumbai Theatre Festival was supposed to start on 12 April 1944. Everything was ready. But on that very day, at around four thirty or five p.m., there was an explosion in the *SS Stikine* which was lying at harbour in the docks. The city was fraught with rumour and tension. That day's show was cancelled but the next day, the house was full. Every seat was taken. The audience seemed totally involved in the play. The festival lasted for ten days. Mama Warerkar told us that the producers had made a profit of one and a half lakh rupees on the whole.

When the explosion took place in the docks, I was acting in a Gujarati play at the Bhangwadi Theatre. We felt a huge thump. We had no idea what had happened. The audience was terrified and the show had to be brought to an end rapidly. Qasimbhai, the producer, sent someone to accompany me home. All down the road, there were clouds of smoke and a feeling of terror. It was only when I got home that Aai relaxed. 'Gosh, Babi, the vessels I had placed on the shelf fell off on their own. I don't know what's going on,' she said. Some people thought that Germany or Japan had attacked India. Slowly the news filtered out that there had been an explosion on board a ship. The areas around Mandvi and Masjid Bunder had taken a direct hit. Many ships had been totally destroyed. We heard that the cause was that the ship had been carrying explosives and cotton. By night, the sky was red.

It did not seem odd then, that even while one area of the city had been levelled, the next day five thousand Marathi people should come to Chowpatty to see a play. But today, this does seem like something extraordinary. Should one say that it is a big city's ability to overcome whatever calamity happens? Or could one say that it is simply an insensitive response? Do we simply not care as long as it has happened to someone else? Do we say to ourselves, 'Let's bother when it turns up on our doorstep'? Wadi Bunder and Mandvi were struggling desperately with the fire. Did that mean that Girgaon, Parel, Grant Road and Worli should stop whatever they were doing? There seems to be no sense in expecting that. One cannot stop the business of living. But must the show go on? When a calamity hits the city, is it right to have film shows or theatrical performances? When we were young we were taught that even a death next door was reason enough to cancel a celebration or a happy event like a Satyanarayan Pooja. But Mumbaikars seem to have slowly begun to forget their obligations to others.

In 1993, a series of explosions rocked the city but the very next day, Mumbai went back to work, seemingly forgetting everything. We seem to be running hard to stay in the same place. People say that this is the love of life you see in Mumbai. But it does seem to have a kind of callousness about it too. The average Mumbaikar lives a life of extraordinary difficulty. When people live like that, humanity begins to seep away. Perhaps it is difficult to say when one changes from being tough-minded to being hard-hearted. Perhaps one does not even know when that happens. Is that what happened to Mumbai? We need a public debate on the issue.

But I have wandered away again. I was telling you about the explosion in the Docks. When something like that happens, many stories are spun around it. Some of them are quite incredible. For instance, one of the stories that became famous at the time was that after the explosion, many of the people living nearby had gold bricks fall into their homes. It was said that one of the ships in the harbour had had gold bars aboard and these had flown out into the air after the explosion. It was said that many people in Mohammed Ali Road, Masjid Bunder, Mandvi and areas around became wealthy overnight. How we wished for a shower of gold in Ramji Purushottam Chawl! Nothing so spectacular ever happened to us. We would continue to live our lives, it seemed, victims of the common certainties of pain and endurance.

*

We knew of one gentleman who worked at the dock. By the grace of God, his life had been spared. Nothing major happened to him but his head was covered with a shower of glass. To begin with the man was half-bald and now this new problem arose. For the next two or three weeks, his wife would be constantly plucking slivers of glass from his hair.

That explosion took place in 1944. We've got ahead of ourselves. We have to go back now to 1942 when an important event took place in the city's history. It should be written in letters of gold in the history text books. This was the year when, at Gowalia Tank, Mahatma Gandhi told the British that it was time to Quit India. The last phase of our battle for freedom had begun. Gandhiji, Pandit Nehru and Sardar Vallabhbhai Patel were all arrested.

The Quit India Movement did not really cause an outburst of anger; the common people continued to live their normal lives but there was also now a new spirit that seemed to move in the city. Students would come out on *prabhat pheris* (dawn processions) and sing songs like '*Kadam kadam badhaaye ja*' (Let us march together) and '*Charkha chala chala ke, lenge swaraaj lenge*' (With every turn of the spinning wheel, we come closer to freedom) and other such patriotic songs. They began to force alcohol shops to close down and also closed down the liquor stills. Women were among the leaders of this movement. There would be public meetings at various places. Jaiprakash Narayan, Dr Ram Manohar Lohia, Aruna Asaf Ali and Achyutrao Patwardhan became the heroes of the youth. Many young couples named their sons Jaiprakash at the time.

My mother was a Gandhian. 'Come rain or shine, in cold weather and hot, with just a shawl over his shoulders, that poor man travels the length and breadth of the country,' she would say with a deep respect. When we were living at Laxmi Chawl, we once had the opportunity of seeing Gandhiji. He was standing in a big open vehicle, his hands folded in a namaste. A huge crowd had gathered at Lamington Road to catch a glimpse of him. We saw him from the gallery of the chawl. He was slight of build but there was an energy in his face. His ears seemed too large for his head. The British police took off their caps as a mark of respect. One or two of the sargeants went down on their knees to welcome him.

I had a great respect for Subhas Chandra Bose. He was a hero to the youth of those days. On the one hand, Gandhiji was preaching ahimsa and on the other, Netaji was saying, 'Give me blood and I will give you freedom.' He aroused enthusiasm in the children. Many young men began to wear round spectacles like Netaji.

At that time, there was also much talk about Captain Laxmi. Netaji had started a women's corps in his Indian National Army. I had read about this somewhere and I thought that I too should join the batallion. It was my age, I suppose, and the passions that go with it. This phase lasted about a month or six weeks. Aai explained things to me: 'Babi, this talk about guns and bullets won't do for us. What if something happens to you over there? What will become of us?'

The educated youth of the city were deeply influenced by Bengal thanks to Netaji, Rabindranath Tagore and New Theatres. The front of the chawl was a narrow long passage with windows that opened onto the outside world. When the women and children got bored of their homes, they would step out into this passage and stare out of it at the world as it went by. My brother Babu would spend hours standing there, singing songs from *Devdas*, *Street Singer* and *Bhakta Purana*. Babu had a fine voice; his favourite singer was K C Dey.

Babu would sometimes come to rehearsals with me. He would sit in a corner and watch. In those days, Altekar had an Alpaca coat. 'I'd like a coat like that,' said Babu. 'Please get one stitched for me.' Eventually he would wear a kurta and lenga but all that, of course, comes much later.

At this point, there's Lakshmibai and her children: Babi, Babu and Kashi. And the Lotlikar family is in trouble. So we'll stop and consider why.

*

My salary at Altekar's was thirty rupees. I was paid by the week. Whenever Dada laid his hands on some money, he would pay us in instalments of ten or fifteen rupees at a time. And then we'd have to wait for the next instalment to come along. We had to make do and actually it was enough for a week. Truth be told, Altekar was paying us what amounted to pocket money for most of the students but the Lotlikars were managing on that much. Since the money didn't come regularly we had to scrimp and save. And expenses were increasing.

When things got desperate, Aai would open her jewellery box, her last resort. When I went the first time to sell some of her jewels to the Pagnis-Petkar jewellery shop, Aai and Babu were miserable. Kashi was in Pune at the time which was all to the good; she didn't have to endure the sight of Aai selling her gold. Piece by piece and with the inevitability of death, Aai's jewellery went to the jewellers, never to return. It had been said in many places, with an air of disgust, that Indian women have a great love of gold. In some ways this is true. Gold is seen as the best investment but that isn't all it means to a woman. It is not just the monetary value alone. It is the traditions that are associated with it, the memories connected to each piece. It is the feeling that many generations of one's family have touched the same pieces.

So Aai's jewellery box was filled with what her family had given her but also with her memories as well. She had held on to her stridhan[1] for many years, protecting it with her life. She must have felt that now our poverty was forcing her to sell her memories. You will probably be shocked at the amount and the variety of the jewellery she had: delicate chains that ran from the earlobe to the top of the ear; gold flowers for the hair in the shapes of roses and frangipani; pearl ear studs, noserings, ear-rings, bracelets and thin bangles, armlets, rings, toe-rings and anklets. That all of them did not get sold was our good luck but we still had to part with many pieces. Aai's medicine cost a great deal of money. Her entire back had lost its skin. In those days, skin creams and lotions were very expensive. We were always afraid of an infection setting in if we did not take the proper precautions. The new skin grew back

[1]Stridhan, a traditional Hindu practice, by which certain property and money was defined as belonging only to a woman. It includes whatever a woman brings with her from her mother's house and what is specifically gifted to her during her lifetime. This may include jewellery, household utensils, saris and suchlike. It is usually passed from mother to daughter.

slowly. Besides the creams and ointments, there were the medicines that had to be taken orally and then there was the money needed for groceries and vegetables and fuel.

Altekar did not pay us all at once. Because of this we were in a trap. Babu was around eighteen or nineteen years old, too young to work. He did try his hand at small jobs here and there but those didn't bring in much money.

The jewellery shop at Pagnis-Petkar was a stone's throw away from our home. It was quite a famous store. Vishnupant Pagnis, who had acted in and as *Sant Tukaram*, often sat at the store. It was a role that had really made him famous. Many people saw him as an avatar of Sant Tukaram. There would be crowds outside the shop, hoping to catch a glimpse of him. I would go to Pagnis-Petkar to sell Aai's jewellery. I had gone there three or four times when Pagnis called me to him and asked me who I was, where I was from and the circumstances that had brought us to the point where I was selling the family jewellery. I told him about acting in *Saraswat* and that I was studying with Altekar. Pagnis was intrigued. Two or three days later, when he met Altekar, he told him about my state and my family's finances—or so I heard later.

'How is she going to manage with your thirty rupees?' he asked. 'Get her a job with some decent money.'

When I heard this I was shocked and frightened. Why did Pagnis have to go and talk to Altekar? Why didn't he tell me about this? What if Dada were to dismiss me? I was in awe of Altekar. For one, he was a man of few words. For another, his personality was somewhat forbidding. In truth, I too had seen Pagnis as a Sant Tukaram-like figure: compassionate and holy. That was why I had told him my story.

But in the next ten or twelve days, Altekar got me a role in a Gujarati play. A private organisation wanted a young woman to play the heroine in a play. They asked Altekar to recommend someone and he suggested my name. One georgette sari, two silver vessels and two hundred and fifty rupees per night (the honorarium for one performance) was fixed. Dada did all the bargaining. There was to be a single performance at Laud Wadi in the Kalbadevi-Bhuleshwar area. The director of the play was Chimanlal Marwadi. He was one of the famous directors of the day. He worked with the Shree Deshi Natak Samaj. Rehearsals in Gujarati theatre lasted for about twenty days. Chimanlal Marwadi worked very hard with me on my dialogue. I did not know much Gujarati so he made me say my dialogues again and again. He told me, 'Sushilaben, when you come for rehearsal, speak to everyone in Gujarati. It's an easy language and you will pick it up quickly.' He was right. In ten or twelve days, I was speaking fairly good Gujarati.

I have always been quick at picking up languages. The play went quite well. I have very little memory of it. I don't even remember its name. In the manner of the time, there was a main storyline and a subsidiary plot. The main storyline was full of melodrama and dramatic tension. The subsidiary plot was comic. There were lot of songs as well. I remember only a few lines.

Chaalo chaalo ne moorat jaaye
Vevaine wadi maa
Aaa Kaako kunwaaro reh jaaye.

Let's go, let's go we will miss the auspicious moment
Let's go to the house of his in-laws
Or the poor man will remain unwed

The audience liked the play and I made my entry into the world of the Shree Deshi Natak Samaj. Chimanlal Marwadi asked me if I would like to join the company. I asked Altekar for his opinion.

'You have a house to run. You will earn good money in that company,' he said.

Altekar's National Theatre Academy (or Little Theatre) was no ordinary theatre company. He wanted to inject new ideas into the world of theatre. If we are to use today's language, one might call *Saraswat* an experimental production. Rangnekar's *Vahini* (Sister-in-law), *Aashirwad* and *Kul-vadhu* had everyone in thrall. That *Saraswat* was not going to be as successful as *Kul-vadhu* was apparent. But neither Mama nor Dada expected it. There was much to learn there, or so I thought. I was not a well-known actress at the time. But I internalised what Altekar had taught me and so I did not embarrass myself on the stage.

Altekar had some basic rules. For instance, you had to know your lines by heart. In the first eight or ten days, you only read the play, sitting around. In other words, you concentrated on the text. When everyone had got their lines straight, we began to block the movements. Altekar would insist on getting each entry and exit exactly right. And so the play began to take shape. Actually, Dada would often forget his copy of the script so he would insist that we should have the play by heart. He would often say that you should be able to say your lines even if you were roused from a deep sleep.

Second, theatre is a collective art form and every actor must keep this in mind when on stage. One's job did not end when one's lines were said. You could not play to the audience for the false coin of individual applause. You should not try and upstage your fellow actors. These were lessons that were drilled into us. Today's actors might learn a thing or two from that, I often feel.

Vijayabai, in the middle period, did train a whole generation of actors. She gave us actors like Nana Patekar, Vikram Gokhale, Suhas Joshi, Nina Kulkarni, Reema Lagoo, Mangesh Kulkarni. If other larger theatre organisations thought to do the same, how much theatre would benefit. In those days many theatre people thought it good sport to mock Altekar and Warerkar. They thought that the Little Theatre produced only over-educated and over-smart actors. They could not see any reason to have such scholars on stage. But later, after Independence, things began to change. The National School of Drama was set up in Delhi. The syllabus there offered a comprehensive perspective on theatre. The State of Maharashtra also began a series of workshops. It is now said that before starting a film or a play, actors often have workshops. This is good news.

Many famous actors such as Durga Khote, Jairaj, David and Mubarak came to meet Dada at the Deodhar Sangeet Vidyalaya. This made us students very happy. They were all well-known and we got to meet them in person. At that time, Durga Khote was very famous. Her father was the well-known solicitor, Laud. He was the legal and financial advisor to Bal Gandharva.

The Saraswat community of Mumbai was proud of the Laud family. Many fanciful stories were told about them. They had usal made of pistachios for breakfast. Their dog had a gold chain around his neck instead of a collar. In the mornings, Durgabai would go horseriding on the

Girgaon back roads. She looked very beautiful then. Both her cheeks had dimples. We kids thought she was like a fairy, descended from the heavens.

Durgabai often came to our Institute. She would talk to Altekar in English. Mubarak, David, Altekar and Durgabai would have long conversations. From time to time, Anant Kanekar would also come to chat with Mama Warerkar about English plays. While all this was going on, Deodhar Master would have brought together all the best musicians who would talk about the grammar of music, the ragas, the techniques. We did not understand much of these conversations but we knew that this was a high level of discourse and we were lucky that it was happening around us. In a certain way, our young minds were being shaped by these experiences. We were being prepared for a life of culture.

These are the ways in which an artist's talents may be cultivated. For art to develop, you need a congenial atmosphere. It helps an actor develop her potential to the full. That this happened to me was because of Mama Warerkar and Altekar. Which was why I loved going to the Little Theatre. While it is true that I did not complete my education, my mother had been right: I learned a lot there. Thanks to the Little Theatre, I developed a deep understanding of theatre and took my place among the knowing and sensitive section of the audience. This was a huge gain for me. But my life as an artist was short-lived. I would have loved to stay longer at the Little Theatre but the conditions at home made that it impossible. I had to enter professional theatre so I could earn our keep.

Altekar's rigorously trained actors were not welcome

in Marathi theatre. It was generally believed that because of his training, we were all a little too big for our boots. Marathi theatrical companies had no desire to hire well-educated or well-trained actors. Natya Niketan and Lalit Kala Darshan were the two most popular companies and both of them had their own stables. It was difficult to get into either. Eventually, I went to the Shree Deshi Natak Samaj which was a Gujarati company and achieved a little success there.

Shree Deshi Natak Samaj was like a Marathi residential theatre company. It was a prestigious institution. It had its own theatre that could seat six hundred to seven hundred people in the Kalbadevi area. Many Gujarati people came to Bombay at the beginning of the nineteenth century to trade or set up small-scale industries. They became traders, shopkeepers, commission agents, brokers, insurance agents, accountants and the like. Kalbadevi, Bhuleshwar-Cowasjee Patel Tank (popularly known as CP Tank), Girgaon, Khetwadi, Thakurdwar, Bora Bazaar were all Gujarati areas. Shree Deshi Natak Samaj was started to provide for the entertainment needs of this community. And it had done its job rather well. It was quite famous in the community. While the plays were entertaining, they were also of a good standard. Shows were held every Wednesday, Saturday and Sunday. Wednesdays were reserved for old plays. Saturdays and Sundays for new productions. If there seemed to be enough demand, there would also be a show on Friday. As the company had its own theatre, it had no problem securing dates. The company had its own *rasoda* (kitchen) that served up to a hundred people in the morning and in the evening.

Everyone ate there, the actors, the musicians, the singers and the director. There were five cooks called *Maharaj*es. Two vegetables, rice with dal, phulkas, farsan, pickle and papads were served. On Sundays, there was also a sweet dish. The meals were subsidized and the cost would be deducted from our salaries. Many of the actors had shifted from Gujarat to Mumbai. The kitchen had been established so that they could get simple home cooking in the city. I never ate at the Shree Deshi Natak Samaj. As soon as the show was over, I would rush home.

The Shree Deshi Natak Samaj was also known as Bhangwadi Theatre[2]. This name came from the wadi in which the theatre was located. The company had an entire floor to itself. It was in a one-storey building. On the ground floor was the auditorium and on the floor above were the rooms reserved for the writers. The writer whose play was on had the right to accommodation there. He would be looked after quite well. No one was allowed to go there except for the bosses. The important actors and the director were the only ones who could ascend.

Prabhulal Dwivedi (1892-1962) was one of the star writers of the company. I acted in two of his plays, *Samay saathe* (In step with time) and *Vadilo na vaanke* (The mistakes of the elders). Dwivedi was of middling stature and quite fat. He wore a jacket over his kurta and dhoti. He didn't say much. He lived on the first floor. There was a mat on the floor on which an immaculate white sheet was spread. There were also some pillows and bolsters, a

---

[2]Bhangwadi because this was where the opium (bhang) markets were traditionally located.

small writing table and a paan supari box. The rest of the floor was covered with mats and dhurries.

When I joined the Shree Deshi Natak Samaj the reins of the company were firmly in the hands of Uttamlakshmiben. After the death of her husband Hargovinddas, she had taken over the business. Uttamlakshmiben kept an eye on everything. She might not have studied much but she was very smart. She knew that theatre was not her forte so she did not interfere with the stories, direction or music. She took care of the company's accounts and its administration. She would be present at every performance. We could see her sitting in the sixth row of the audience—a powerful presence.

The Shree Deshi Natak Samaj's plays were very popular. Many of the leading traders and important people would come to see them with their families. One of the reasons for this was the spotless reputation of the company. Its name had never been associated with any wrongdoing. It was known for its good clean entertainment.

Samay saathe was my first play with the company. If I may use the language of the time, I had the role of the side heroine. In the play, my hero was played by an actor called Chunibhai. The lead hero was Qasimbhai. He was also the director. Motiben was the lead heroine. She was very beautiful; she was fair, tall and had a musical voice. Let me tell you about Qasimbhai and Motiben. There was a rumour about Motiben at the time. It was said that she used to sell *datun*—neem twigs used to clean the teeth—at Kalbadevi. Gujarati people are known for their dependence on *datun* and so she was selling these twigs, calling out '*Ek paisa ma leela leyi lo*' (One paisa only, take them now) as Hargovindbhai's car passed up and down the road every day. This was where he is supposed to have discovered her and made her a star.

It was said that Motiben was totally illiterate. She would take the script and sit down with it and pretend to read. She would follow whatever Qasimbhai told her to the letter. Turn the page, he would say and she would turn the page. She would run her finger over each line. After about eight to ten days, she would know the entire thing by heart. Once she was dressed and made up she looked very beautiful. She would make Meena Kumari or Madhubala look ordinary in comparison.

She was from the Gujarati Gosai caste. The Gosais are known to be good at singing and acting. They were a nomadic community that travelled about presenting traditional theatre to audiences. The Meers were the Muslim equivalent. They shared the same lot in life and so there was no difference made between Hindus and Muslims. A Muslim boy played Anusuya in an *aakhyaan* (a dramatized story) about Sati Anusuya. They understood each other because they followed the same vocation. This was why religion was not a problem. Qasimbhai, for instance, seemed to be a Muslim in name only. His lifestyle was Hindu as was his behaviour and general practices. Motibai worked in Ranjit Natak Company in Saurashtra. The company came to Mumbai and gave a performance at the Bhangwadi Theatre. Qasimbhai and Hargovinddas were present at this folk performance and asked her to join the Shree Deshi Natak Samaj. They say this is how she became a heroine in the company. So the story about her selling datun was just that—a story. But then there are thousands of these tales told in the world of the arts. What is true is that Motibai was one of the most famous actors of her time and the Greta Garbo of the Shree Deshi Natak Samaj.

Motibai was the heroine of all the plays. My songs in *Samay saathe* were set to music by Hajibhai, Qasimbhai's younger brother. The tabla, the organ and the violin were the accompaniments. The basic message of the play was that one has to move with the times. If one falls behind the times, there is not much point to life. The play was, in a way, quite modern but it was simple in its presentation. There was not much tension or melodrama in it. It was supposed to be an entertaining play. What had to be said was said in a light-hearted manner. The greatest attention was paid to the costumes. Everyone was dressed in fine clothes, zari-laden saris for all the ladies, and lots of jewellery. There were a good many songs and jokes. Chhagan Romeo was a famous actor with the Shree Deshi Natak Samaj. There was not a single actor on the Gujarati stage to compete with him when it came to comedy. Chhagan Romeo was lean, of medium height and dark. He had a flexible body he could twist into a series of curious shapes. He had the same position in Gujarati theatre as Dinkar Kamanna Dhere and, at a later time, Baban Prabhu had on the Marathi stage. He simply had to make an entry and the applause would break out. He had a trademark entry for each play. The main story always had a comic subplot and because of Chhagan Romeo, these comic scenes were very popular.

The responsibility of bringing the audience back to the main storyline lay with Motibai. *Samay saathe* did very well. There were many shows and every show was 'housefull'. Each song would get at least three or more encores. This meant that if the show started at four in the evening, it would only end at around eleven in the night. One of my songs was a great favourite with audiences:

> *Aage aage kyaank thandi lheri*
> *Kyaank chhaaya gheri*
> *Jeevanpanthe jaata jaata*

This meant that as a man walks down the road of life, he may enjoy cool pleasant breezes at some places but there are also times when he must meet with deep shadows. The tune of the song was very simple. Although we had many performances every week, Qasimbhai insisted on a complete rehearsal and so we kept the standard of the performances very high. I was now a salaried employee of the Shree Deshi Natak Samaj. The system of being paid on a nightly basis came later. I was earning three hundred and fifty rupees a month. The year: 1944-45. Motibai's salary was one thousand two hundred rupees. She had a Baby Austin too.

Three hundred and fifty rupees a month was a fortune for us. I managed to buy my mother a gold chain and diamond-studded bangles. I bought Kashi a gold chain too and studs for her ears. We were seeing good days. Our little home at the Ramji Purushottam Chawl was full of happiness. My brother taught me to sign my name in English. He told me that it would make a good impression if I did so. His English was very good. He could solve *The Times of India* crossword in twenty minutes. Now Ambarish, my son, follows in his footsteps.

My mother and I had a joint account at the Saraswat Bank at Girgaon. I was now an income tax assessee but we did not become arrogant because I was earning some money. Let me tell you a story. I began to wear high-heeled sandals which made a tick-tock sound when I walked. Samrath Bhaiyya, the caretaker of our chawl, told my mother, 'Your daughter is now walking around with a lot of pride. This is not a good thing.' My mother said to me, 'Today Samrath is saying this. Tomorrow others will say it too. People should not say that you have become high and mighty because you have become successful and made some money. As it is, there are enough misunderstandings about actors. You need to be as simple as possible in your behaviour. There is no need for style of this kind.'

I bade farewell to the high-heeled sandals and began to wear Kolhapuri slippers instead. Sometimes I also wore mojdis.

*

After *Samay saathe*, I began to work in *Vadilo na vaanke*. This was an old successful play at the Shree Deshi Natak Samaj. The main story line was about how the younger generation of a family had to bear the consequences of the mistakes made by previous generations. Motibai and Qasimbhai were the main characters. I was the side heroine and Chunibhai was my opposite number. The music was by Hajibhai. The play ran well. There were lots of songs, *dohe*, *shaayri* and poems of four lines each. And so the play often ran for four or five hours. The audience loved the songs and poems. The theme was modern and novel.

The author was on the side of the young. The youth at the time often felt that their lives were being trampled upon. The Second World War was coming to an end. People believed that a new world order was about to begin and so *Vadilo na vaanke* benefitted greatly from this.

The atmosphere in Mumbai was charmed. There was rationing of foodgrain and everywhere people were beginning to feel the pinch of rising prices; yet because Independence seemed so near the mood was also festive. We could see the change in the behaviour of the English policemen. On some of their faces, it was possible to see traces of anxiety about their future. Then the naval ratings mutinied and Mumbai was all agog.

'Now the British are going to find it difficult to continue to rule here. They will have to leave,' Anna Chaudhury would say to my mother.

'Never mind,' my mother would reply.

Anna Chaudhury was deeply interested in national as well as international politics. He would tell Aai and Babu all about what was happening. He knew that India was going to be independent but Partition came as a surprise. Someone came and told us that many of the houses on Mohammed Ali Road were sporting flags with the green crescent moon and star on them. The residents of the chawl were horrified. They wanted nothing to do with this Partition business. Aai would ask rhetorically, 'Does a nation break into pieces like that?' This question is still with me today. Was it really impossible to prevent Partition and if such a division had to happen, should it not have been made with some forethought and some preparation? That it was done in such a terrible hurry meant that those who suffered most were the ordinary people. Independence came with a sob in its throat and blood on its hands.

*

It was around this time that small changes began to happen in Mumbai. New buildings came up, each with three or four storeys, with three or four flats to a floor. The toilet and bathroom were now inside the house. One of the special features of these new houses was the spacious balconies outside. Women began to wear five-yard saris. The nine-yard sari began a slow fade-out. In these new five-yard saris, women set out to work. The men began to wear trousers and shirts. Now people went to work around nine or nine-thirty in the morning and came back in the evening. More and more people listened to the radio and read the newspapers. Education increased in importance. Many private schools were opened.

The rains came to Mumbai between the seventh and fourteenth of June. This was also the time when schools began. There was no shortage of books in the shops, the examination timetables were never messed up, question papers did not leak and the results were always declared on time. The Municipal sanitation workers never went on strike on the first day of the rains. The city operated well and on time. The hands of the clock ruled us all. This was the discipline by which Mumbai lived.

I began to work with companies other than the Shree Deshi Natak Samaj. After all, there were two or three days at a stretch when there were no shows. What sense did it make to be sitting at home, doing nothing? HMV asked if I would like to work with them. They were bringing out short gramophone records for the rural sector. The topics were things like farming, sowing and watering crops, all presented in crisp dialogue. I met some interesting and talented people there: the poet G D Madgulkar, the music director Sudhir (Babuji) Phadke, Vasantrao Kamerkar, head of HMV's light music section, and G N Joshi, the singer, composer and recording executive who worked with HMV, among others. Madgulkar's language was exquisite. He knew hundreds of poems, *dohe* and the like by heart. One felt as if he were holding Saraswati Aai's little finger as he walked into the HMV office. Babuji's music was extremely beautiful. The HMV office was somewhere in the Fort area. There was a restaurant close by to which we all went from time to time. We would split the bill.

At around this time, I also worked in two Marathi plays. Master Vinayak Rao asked me to act in *Usna nowra* (Husband on loan). He had come to see me with Bal Sathe, the violinist. (Or was it Nana Sathe? I no longer remember.) If my memory serves me right, Master Vinayak lived in Kumud Villa on Lamington Road.

Usna nowra ran for two shows. Rehearsals were held at a hall in Shenvi Wadi. That was where I saw Lata Mangeshkar for the first time. Lata is now well-known all over the world. She has success, popularity and fame but she has earned it all on the basis of her hard work and talent. When someone says her name, I immediately recall the Lata I knew in those days. She was thin with thick long curly hair, a straight nose, a dark complexion and bright eyes. She spoke very little but laughed a lot. She might have looked ordinary but her face glowed with vitality.

At that time, many Marathi girls had come into the film industry because of family conditions that required them to earn their livings. Some were in cinema and others in theatre. We would meet each other from time to time. We let each other know when there was work available. Shalini Mardolkar, Baby Alka (Achrekar), the Rane sisters (Kavita and Gaandhari), the Fenani sisters (Sarla and Hema), Madhubala Chawla, Heera Sawant, Sulochana Kadam, Mogal Pitale (who became Mangala Sanzgiri after she married), Nalini Nagpurkar (who was a bit senior to all of us). These are some of the names I remember. We knew each other to a lesser or greater degree but we kept in touch and we had some fellow feeling for each other. Some of us went on to become quite famous. Lata, for instance, became a legend in her lifetime. Others achieved success in different measures. After marriage, I gave up the stage. For the next twenty years, I was totally involved in the world of my family and children and yet I remember these names.

In 1974, Shivshahir Shree Babasaheb Purandare mounted a programme at Shivaji Park called *Shivrajyabhishek* (The Coronation of Shivaji). It ran for a month. The backstage was handled by Damu Kenkre and Arvind Deshpande. Kenkre asked me to take charge of the costumes and help backstage. It was a spectacular festival. Through the month that we were there, Lata Mangeshkar would often come with her family to see the show. Once I even met with her. She spoke kindly to me and asked after my family. There was no false pride in her; she did not behave badly at all. Even today, she remains the same. When my son goes to meet her, she asks after me. God grant her even more good things in her life.

Altekar had warned me that I should never think of joining the movies but once I did go to Ranjit Movietone as I had been called there. Babu and Aai were with me. Ranjit was a well-known company at the time. Chandulal Shah was its owner. They made so many films that they were known as a cinema factory. Babu, Aai and I were waiting to be called. A gentleman of our acquaintance was supposed to take us to meet the man in charge of the studio. He was late and so we were waiting for him, sitting outside in the heat.

Just then Noor Mohammed Charlie came in. He was a well-known comedian of the time. He asked my mother what we were doing there. When she explained, he said to her, 'Don't sit and wait like this. Go home right now. This is a terrible world, sick at heart. Continue in the theatre. Don't dream about cinema.' Then he got into his car and left. We left, too. Babu said, 'Babi, I am glad we got out of there. I didn't feel right about it.'

The odd thing was that in 1944, Altekar had asked me if I would like to go to Madras to act in a film. Uday Shankar, a famous dancer, was planning an ambitious film, *Kalpana*. He would choreograph it himself but Altekar was in charge of the acting. Shankar needed some young men and women to act in the film. It was a shoot that would last six to eight months. It was not possible for me to leave Mumbai for such a long period. Dada realised that I had a lot going on in Mumbai at the time. Finally, he sent Bapurao Marathe with his two daughters to Madras. One of them was Usha Marathe. She would become the famous Usha Kiran later.

At Shree Deshi Natak Samaj, I met two sisters, Vatsala

and Vijaya. We became good friends. Both of them acted in Deshi's plays. They were Shreedhar Deshmukh's daughters. There was a third sister as well. Both Vatsala and Vijaya were tall, thin and pretty. They both understood acting well and were really good at comedy. Both were also good natured. When there were afternoon rehearsals or shows, we would feast on moong bhajiyas, available in the cortner shop which sold sev-ghatia too.

Vijaya Deshmukh went on to join Rajkamal and changed her name to Sandhya. *Jhanak jhanak paayal baaje*, *Do aankhen baarah haath*, *Navrang*, *Jal bin machhli nritya bin bijli* were some of her well-known films. People admired her dancing. Vatsala also acted in some films and achieved some success. Both of them supported the family.

*

Shree Deshi Natak Samaj had many peculiarities. Each play would have a garba in it. Ten to twelve pretty little boys would be chosen to dance. They would be dressed in pretty parkar-polkas of different colours. Once they began to twirl and swirl, you could imagine that several variously coloured flames were dancing on the stage. Needless to say the audience loved it. Once they were done, these boys would strip down to their undershorts and vests and help the actors. One of their main jobs was to bring us buckets of warm water with which we bathed. A bucket of warm water cost eight annas. At the end of the month, these boys would have earned about thirty to forty rupees, perhaps even a little more. They would send twenty to thirty rupees home.

There was a tradition by which every actor who earned

more than three hundred rupees a month had to feed the entire company once a year. When it fell to my turn, the hot weather was upon us. Aamras puri was one of the dishes on the menu. When lunch was served, it was announced two or three times: 'This meal is courtesy Sushilaben.' The meal was much appreciated.

Another tradition was that of the benefit night. It was meant to honour an actor. But this was no hollow honour. Whatever was collected would be given to the actor along with flowers, a shawl and other customary offerings. To have a benefit night was seen as a big honour.

I left the company before I could have a benefit night. There was no real reason behind my departure. It was just that I was bored. Qasimbhai tried two or three times to get me to change my mind but I was determined to leave.

Looking back now, I can see that Shree Deshi Natak Samaj had as much of a role to play in the shaping of me as an actor as Parshwanath Altekar or Mama Warerkar. I feel much gratitude towards it. The actor is like a machine. The machine has to be kept working. There were many performances of *Vadilo na vaanke* and *Samay saathe*. *Samay saathe*, in particular, was very popular. But I was acting all the time so I didn't get a chance to get rusty.

I was quite famous thanks to Shree Deshi Natak Samaj. I was once interviewed for Badri Kaanchwalla's monthly magazine *Chitrapat*. I even made it to the cover. A director asked me whether I would work in Gujarati pictures. I refused the offer. *Chitrapat* was popular among the Gujaratis. Badri Kaanchwalla was married to Amirbai Karnataki, the famous playback singer. Shree Deshi Natak Samaj also had a certain prestige. One day I went to sing in the chorus of a film made by Prakash Pictures. The lead singer was Amirbai Karnataki. After the recording when we were being served refreshments, Shankarbhai Bhatt came up to me. He and his brother, Vijaybhai Bhatt, were the owners of Prakash Pictures. He said, 'Sushilaben, you are an artiste with Shree Deshi Natak Samaj. You are a second heroine there. You have achieved some fame and the company too has a good reputation. You should not be singing in the chorus.' I never went to sing in the chorus again. I did not feel it was demeaning to sing in a chorus nor do I think so today. Many of my friends sang in the chorus. Some achieved a measure of success. It is said that music directors would hold up recordings until the Rane sisters arrived. But I was now associated with the Shree Deshi Natak Samaj. I did not want to do anything that would damage its reputation. So I decided not to sing in the chorus again.

That the audience gets pleasure out of a performance is a source of great joy for any actor. This joy cannot be measured in monetary terms. In that sense an artist is like a bird carrying seeds on its wings. As it flies some of these seeds fall to the earth. Some dry up, others are swallowed by the earth. Of course, there were also dense viewers who would see a play like *Aandhlaachya shaala* (School for the blind) and say something like, 'But where are the blind people?' They are still around though perhaps there were fewer then. Some seeds are wasted. But some take root. The artist sows a seed and a tree may grow there. Most ordinary educated viewers understand a certain standard of performance. Which is why films like *Sant Tukaram*, *Maanus*, *Shejaari*, *Koonkoo*, and plays like Acharya Atre's

Gharabaher and *Udyaacha sansar* or *Satteche ghulam* and *Saraswat* by Mama Warerkar and *Kul-vadhu* by M G Rangnekar have been widely appreciated.

Here is a memory that surfaces suddenly. Shree Deshi Natak Samaj was in Bhaangwadi. On the corner of the wadi, there was a footwear shop. Not much of a shop really, a stall one might say. An elderly man ran the stall. One day, he presented me with a pair of brand-new chappals. They were plain but strongly built and had a thin strap running around the heel.

'Tai, I saw your play yesterday,' he said. 'I don't know much Gujarati but your songs are sweet on the ear. You have a great skill but I have one too. So I made you this pair of chappals.' I used those chappals for a couple of years.

A little way from our chawl was the shop of a Gujarati tailor. He saw me in *Samay saathe*. He came to me and said, 'Sushilaben, give me one of your blouses. I will stitch four blouses for you. You don't have to pay a paisa for the cloth or stitching. How well you acted! No one could have said you're from a Marathi family at all.'

Today, actors are well-respected in our society. From politicians to college principals, from scientists to industrialists, everyone seems to have a lot of time for actors and singers. Cricketers too have become celebrities. Perhaps it is time for all these people to recognize that they have to behave with some responsibility.

At one point in time, political leaders had a great effect on the people. Pandit Nehru, Sardar Patel and Jaiprakash Narayan and in a later time Lal Bahadur Shastri and Indira Gandhi won the people's respect and admiration. Raj Kapoor and Dilip Kumar were their equivalents in the world of cinema. Things are very different now, the leaders run around after actors and actresses and cricketers. At such a time, people can only hope that the actors will behave in a manner that befits their new influence.

My Mishra Marriage

When I left the Shree Deshi Natak Samaj, I got a Marwadi play called *Ramu Chanana* by Bharat Vyas who would later become a successful lyricist in Hindi cinema. The famous song, '*Ae maalik tere bande hum*' (O Lord, we are your servants) from *Do aankhen baarah haath* was written by Vyas. He was originally from Rajasthan. According to the tradition of the Marwadi community, he went to Calcutta to study. There he finished a degree in commerce and joined the theatre movement. Calcutta had a very strong Marwadi community that ran all the industries. They were also great patrons of music and theatre. There were also many Parsi theatre companies in the city. Bharat Vyas wrote *Ramu Chanana* and presented it there. It was hugely appreciated. After a while, Vyas decided to present his play in Mumbai so he packed his scripts and his costumes and lugged his trunks here. He cast his brother, Brijmohan Vyas (known as B M Vyas) as the hero. I was the heroine. Actually Bharat Vyas wanted the heroine from Calcutta to reprise her role in Mumbai. Her name was also Sushila but the Marwadi community of Mumbai insisted I should be cast. Many aficionados of Marwadi theatre were regulars at the Bhangwadi Theatre. One of them was a man called Roongta. 'Take Sushila

Lotlikar in your play. She acts well and has a sweet voice,' he told Vyas. Vyas did not know me personally. One day someone brought a message from Roongta and so I went to meet Bharat Vyas in Jamnadas Pacheria's house. Pacheriaji was then a famous Marwadi playwright and author. He was also mad about theatre. He would watch all the plays of Bal Gandharva, Lalit Kala Darsha and Natyaniketan with delight. He lived in Fanaswadi, Girgaon. His house was in a chawl but it had large rooms and high ceilings. There was a public hall where we rehearsed the play. The rates were fixed at three hundred fifty rupees for the first night and two hundred fifty for every following night. Bharat Vyas gave me my lines written separately. They were in Rajasthani, a completely new language for me.

Aai said to me, 'Babi, now what have you taken on? What is to become of you?' I did not reply. In one way she was right. But I was not going to refuse just because I had not done it before. I believe you should try everything once and if you succeed, well and good.

We rehearsed for about three weeks. It took me some time to get used to the Marwadi language. Bharat Vyas worked really hard with me. He taught me the inner music of the Rajasthani language. In all, *Ramu Chanana* has about thirty songs. All of these had been written and composed by Vyas. I had five or six solos in addition to which the hero and I had duets and then there were dohe, poems and several four-line songs. Accompanying us were Mohan Kalla on the organ and a violinist called Tilak. In addition there were dholkis and tablas for percussion.

'Get the songs right. The play succeeded in Calcutta because of the songs,' Bharat Vyas told me.

Ramu Chanana is a traditional Rajasthani legend like Heer-Ranjha or Bajirao-Mastani. It is the story of star-crossed lovers whose relationship is not consummated. These two young people, whose love is forbidden and whose lives are cut short, touched a chord with Rajasthani audiences. Ramu is a sonar (a goldsmith and therefore of a lower caste) while his beloved Chanana is from a high-caste Thakur family. The high walls of their different backgrounds stand between the lovers. Unable to bear the pain of being parted, they kill themselves. This is the short version. There are many variants of the story all over India and they are all very popular. The audience seems to get a great thrill out of these stories of unsuccessful love. Hindi films are full of couples who die and these films are always successful. Because of its powerful writing, the quality of its acting, the lavishness of its costumes and its mellifluous music, *Ramu Chanana* became a tremendous hit. There was a show every Sunday at the Bhangwadi Theatre. In the afternoon, they would have a Gujarati play that would wind up by about seven o'clock. Then *Ramu Chanana* would come on at eight o'clock and go on until one-thirty or two am. This continued for about one-and-a-half years. The play had its fair share of repeat audiences as well. Once the songs started, the audience settled down to listen with delight. I offer a few examples:

Kab se khadi hoon tore dwaar
Bula le mohe Ramu-re
Ramu jharokhe se jhaank le
To main itna keh doon
Khol de mann ke dwaar.
Bule le mohe Ramu-re.

I have been standing at your door for so long
Oh Ramu my love, call me to you
Oh Ramu, look out of the window
So that I may be allowed to say this much
Open the door of your heart to me
Oh Ramu, call me to you

There was another:

Mhaari nazar tadpaawe
Jeeyo jalaave
Chit chaave
Meethi boliyaan man bhaave
Ghani suhaave
Chanana pher milaanga (3)
Ramu pher milaanga (3)
Bharoso mhaaro raakhi Ramu
Tu Thakur ki deekri
Main hoon ek sonar
Thaari mhaari preetdi
Ya kis bidh lagasi paar?
Chanana pher milaanga (3)
Bharoso mhaari raakhi Chanana.

My eyes pine for you
My heart yearns for you
My soul longs for you
I leave you many sweet words
To please the mind
Chanana, we will meet again
Ramu, we will meet again
Have faith in your Ramu
You're the daughter of a Thakur

I am only a goldsmith
How then shall our love
Surpass these borders?
Chanana, we will meet again
Chanana, keep the faith

'*Shaalu hirwa, paachuni madwa, veni tipedi*[1] *ghaala*' (In a green sari, decked with emerald jewellery, her hair bound in a braid of three strands) was an Usha Mangeshkar song penned by Shanta Shelke. It was based on *Chanana pher milaanga*. There are great similarities between both the songs but this could just be because of the traditional nature of both the songs.

Ramu Chanana has a sad ending. First Ramu sacrifices his life and when Chanana hears about this, she dresses herself up in all her finery and kills herself. But before that she sings this song:

Sun ri sakhi, tose kahoon
Main mere mann ki baat ri
Jaati hoon Ramu se milne
Is ghadi, is saathi ri.
Chahe andheri raat ho
Barse chaahe barsaat ri
Aakhir ko milan hai so
Sau baat ki ek baat ri.

Listen, my friend, as I tell you
The secrets of my heart.

---

[1]Tipedi had three strands, paanchpedi had five and on very special occasions a woman might tie her hair in a saatpedi with seven strands. Each increase in the number meant a corresponding increase in the tightness of the braid.

I am now off to meet my Ramu
In the moment that we part
What if the night be dark and gloomy?
Or if the rain comes pelting down
I will go to my loved one
That is all that matters to me

When the song was done, Chanana (played by me) would commit suicide. But the audiences loved the song and would demand that I sing it again. So I would have to put aside my stage death and come to life again and sing it again. This happened three or four times. Finally, at one of the shows, the writer Bharat Vyas came on stage and said to the audiences: 'Here is Chanana embracing death and you are whistling and insisting on encores? Can't you see how serious the matter is?'

But an even more serious matter was happening on-stage. After their death Ramu (B M Vyas) and Chanana meet in heaven. This is the last scene of the play. At the top of the stage, near the proscenium arch, were tied two wooden planks. We had to climb up to these using rope ladders. These were the kind you see in army training camps. We had about two minutes to climb the ladders and seat ourselves on the planks and then the curtain would rise again and we would wave to the audiences and sing our '*Pher melaanga, pher melaanga*' song again. The organ and the violin would be playing other-worldly music all the time. We would join hands in 'heaven' and wave to the audience. This was a great hit with the viewers who were relieved to know that even if we had not resolved our differences on Earth, we were together in heaven. Then they would all go back to their own world, riven by caste, creed, community and religion. When the curtain fell a last time, I could come down from heaven and the show would be over. It was a relief that there were no encores for this song or I would have been scrambling up ladders again to start my heavenly waving. In the beginning, I was terrified of the ladder. Bharat Vyas said to me, 'Sushilaben, don't worry. Just do it five or six times and you'll get used to it.' Two or three backstage hands would steady the ladder as I went up and down. It was tiring but I did get used to it.

Once Prithviraj Kapoor came to see *Ramu Chanana*. He looked at the rope ladder contraption and said, 'Vyas, is this a play or a circus?' He told me and B M Vyas, 'Children, be careful when you go up and down. Don't break your bones.' Prithviraj-ji invited me to work with him in Prithvi Theatres but I had to refuse. *Ramu Chanana* was doing very well and there were many shows. I was the heroine of the play. Besides Prithvi had its own female actors in Azra and Uzra.

Mama Warerkar also came to see *Ramu Chanana*. He was curious about plays in other languages; and I was acting in this one. Afterwards, he came backstage. I touched his feet and he said, 'Babi, must say you make a fine Marwadi girl. You've planted a flag of the Konkan in Rajasthan!'

Today I believe that my roots are in Goa. My hometown is in Ratnagiri and I grew up in Mumbai. I'm a child of the coasts but I had now begun to play in the sands of Rajasthan. This is how destiny shapes our geography. You have to keep on moving and try not to complain too much.

While I was acting in *Ramu Chanana*, I had the good fortune of meeting Shanta Apte at the Circo Film

Company. I had gone there on some work and I was told that she was also on the premises. I asked to meet her. She was very kind and affectionate as she spoke to me. I told her about *Ramu Chanana* and that I had studied a little with Altekar. She said the most important thing for an artiste is to do her own make up. I told her that I did my own. Then she warned me that producers are often unwilling to pay you what is your due. She told me, 'Before you sit down to do your make up, you must ask about your money. If necessary, say that you won't put on your make-up until you're paid. That's when everyone will fall into line.' She asked me when the next show was and where. 'I'll see if I can come for it,' she said. And right enough, over the next couple of weeks, she did come and see *Ramu Chanana*. The audience began to murmur and mutter. Shantabai looked every inch the star. There was a great hauteur in her face but she could fell a grown man at six paces. She said to Bharat Vyas, 'I have come to see Sushila perform.' As she left she said to me: 'You are getting your money on time, aren't you?' It is important for me to note here that Mr Vyas never once refused to pay my money. As soon as I sat down to do my makeup, my payment for the night would be on my table.

Chanana's costume was a heavy one. It was supposed to be an eighty-panel ghagra. It had been stitched specially for the show. It's now I believe a common phrase in Rajasthan— '*assi kalano ghagra*'. Three were stitched for me. With it, I wore a full-sleeved blouse. Then came a jacket that reached my waist and on top of that an odhni. The blouse and the jacket had tassels at various places. Chanana is supposed to be a rich landlord's daughter. This meant she would be fond of good clothes and jewellery. On both hands, she wore bracelets. From wrist to elbow, she wore gold bangles. They were really silver but gold plated. They were tight near the wrist and slightly loose above. They were not like the green glass bangles that married Maharashtrian girls wear. These are the ornaments that an unmarried woman wears in Rajasthan. Her fingers would be covered with several rings. Around her neck, a necklace as thick as a garland and in her ears, large dangling ear-rings. On her forehead, a bindi and around her upper arm, an armlet; anklets on her feet. Vyas had hired a Rajasthani woman to get me ready for the shows. After each show, she would also help me undress and put away all the jewellery safely for some of the ornaments were made of gold. The ghagra was of a thin soft material. There was another material used inside. Vyas had spent a lot of money on *Ramu Chanana*. The entire look was stylish and aristocratic. But he also made lots of money on the show.

Ramu Chanana ran for two to two-and-a-half years at the Bhangwadi theatre. Then the Gujarati audience also began to come to see it. This did not go down well with the Shree Deshi Natak Samaj. They must have felt that we were cutting into their audiences. It was not as though there was any real competition between Marwadi and Gujarati theatre. Vyas had only brought this play to Mumbai to prove that he could succeed here as well. But if you look at it carefully, you can see that there isn't much difference between the culture of the two states of Rajasthan and Gujarat. When you listen to the folk songs of Kutch and Saurashtra, they bring to mind the songs of Rajasthan.

Both states revel in colour. Sunshine yellow, blood red, leaf green are the favoured hues. These colours were all on display in *Ramu Chanana*.

In the interval, many of the members of the audience would come backstage to see us in the flesh, as it were. That was enough for them. That I was a Marathi girl and spoke Marwadi was a matter of great interest. Some women would bring us things to eat, their servants carrying the food in huge dabbas. Others would bring their jewellery boxes and put them in my hands. 'Please wear my jewellery on stage in the last scene,' they would ask. I was terrified that I might lose their jewellery but they would reassure me that their servants would be standing in the wings waiting to collect the ornaments as soon as the show was over. And so it was that I came to wear many of the priceless ornaments of the Marwadi community on stage. It was my good luck nothing ever got lost. 'For Ramu, you give up your life,' more than one woman said to me. 'What does it matter if our jewellery goes missing?' Often the average person in the audience cannot tell the difference between a character and the real person who plays the role.

Let me tell you a story about the film *Ram Rajya*. It was an extremely successful film. Prem Adib played Ram and Shobhna Samarth played Sita. When she was on the set with full make-up on, Shobhna looked every inch a Sita, chaste and pure. On the first day of shooting, after the shot was okayed, Shobhnabai sat down and lit a cigarette. They say that the producer-director Vijaybhai Bhatt was shocked to see this. Now Bhatt-sahib knew that Shobhna Samarth was Sita as long as the shot lasted and she stepped out of character as soon as it was over but still he was shocked. And if this can happen to such an experienced director, can you imagine what goes on in the mind of an average viewer?

But the audience is a strange animal indeed. The Gujarati audience is an energetic, enthusiastic one that offers a great deal of support when you are on stage. Some may even spout an Urdu couplet which seems apposite. When the comedy routines began in *Samay saathe* the laughter broke out in great uncontrollable waves. When a sad or tense sequence was on, the audience would get into the spirit of what was happening on stage. In comparison, the Rajasthani audience was more decent and behaved with more grace. They responded, but in a controlled fashion.

My second Marwadi play was *Magarmachh* (Crocodile). When the Bhangwadi Theatre refused permission to stage *Ramu Chanana*, the play had to close down after a nearly two-year run. This was because the Rajasthani community lived largely in the Kalbadevi-Bhuleshwar-Thakurdwar-C P Tank area and so the Bhangwadi Theatre was really the best place for Marwadi plays. There was no point in putting one on in Damodar Hall, Parel. And so Bharat Vyas decided to close down. But its unparalleled success gave Marwadi Theatre in the city a huge boost. Other plays like *Aakdya pan padya koni* (I bowed but did not fall) and *Nayi bindhni* (The new nose-ring/The new bride) were also hits.

In the past few pages I have already mentioned Pandit Jamnadas Pacheria. He was a leading playwright in Marwadi theatre. He was deeply respected by Marathi and Hindi playwrights and directors too. I have also mentioned that rehearsals for *Ramu Chanana* happened in Fanaswadi. Pacheria's wife had a fondness for me. Both of them would feed me Rajasthani delicacies. It was in her hall that rehearsals took place. It was truly a hall. Forty people could sit there comfortably, it was so spacious. Along all the four walls were cupboards full of books. Every cupboard had 'The Jamnadas Pacheria Library' painted on it. Pacheria's bibliophilia had cost his wife a great deal. 'Send him to the marketplace to buy vegetables and he will come back with a bag of books,' the poor thing would say. His daughters were called Savitri and Lalita. Because they were born after so many years, both husband and wife loved their daughters very much. They were also very clever girls.

It was Pacheria who told me about *Magarmachh*. He asked me if I would like to act in the play as the heroine. 'Big house, hollow foundations' summed up the play. Its message was: Too great a love for money can damage human relationships.

Pandit Indra was the writer of *Magarmachh*. He was originally from Rajasthan. In the 1940s, he had achieved much fame as a lyricist. He had written songs for films like *Tansen*, *Man ki Jeet* and *Mr Sampat*. *Nani, teri morni ko mor le gaye/Baaki jo bacha tha saare chor le gaye* (Granny, your peahen has been whisked off by a peacock/The rest thieves have looted: barrel, lock and stock) was a famous children's song from *Masoom* (1960). It was sung by Hemant Kumar's daughter. Pandit Indra wore a dhotar, a dagla and a black topi on his head. He was remarkably simple. He said very little. He suffered from asthma and the cold weather and the rains would set him off. His chest would heave like the bellows in an iron forge. He would wrap himself up and try to sleep it off. Pandit Indra and

Pacheria directed *Magarmachh*. Rehearsals went on for about six weeks and they gave me a separate script with my lines. I had them by heart in the next fifteen to twenty days. Kshirode Bhattacharya, a young Bengali music director, did a great job with the music. All the songs were set to traditional tunes. Pandit Indra taught these to Kshirode Babu who refined them a little. I remember one of the songs from the play:

Aaj mhane aaj mhane mitho mitho soopno aayo, eh Ma
Sapno mein saaybo risaayo, eh Ma
Baagaa maa ramteene saatheeye uthaayi
Saathneeya soo mhaari preetdi chhudaayi
Aaj mhaase, aaj mhaase jora jori nehlādaa
Lagaayo, eh Ma
Pyaaro pyaaro piharyo chhudaayo, eh Ma.

The song tells the story of a young woman whose marriage preparations are in full swing. She says that she had had a beautiful dream in which her beloved, her husband-to-be, got angry with her unexpectedly. She was in a garden playing with her friends when he suddenly arrived and tried to approach her. She says that he took her away from her parents and her friends but she had felt she would have to go with him. The tune was simple and sweet. Its Rajasthani flavour had been set beautifully by Kshirode Bhattacharya. This song was very popular, especially with the women in the audience. There were always two or three encores in every show.

Pandit Murlidhar Dadhich came for the rehearsals. He was a fine poet and his plays in Marwadi were very popular. He was Pandit Indra's cousin on the paternal side. He was thin and tall and in indifferent health. He too wore a dhotar, dagla and a black topi on his head. His expression was funereal but his sense of comedy, his comic timing was brilliant. He was a charming person and had a great knowledge of Rajasthan folk music. One of the songs Pandit Dadhich taught me went like this:

Binjaara re...chet chet kar chaal
Chaaron ore chor lutere! Loot na le thhora maal
Chet chet kar chaal.
Koi saloni thaar saage
Piya ne bhejo sandeso
Ban-jungle bhoolan bhatkan ko
Man mein bhaari andeso
Chet chet kar chaal
Binjaara, chet chet kar chaal.

Walk with care, traveller, walk with care
Thieves surround you everywhere
Make sure you walk with care
Someone who loves you
Sends you this warning
As you wander through the wilds
With profound thoughts dawning
Make sure you walk with care
Traveller, make sure you walk with care

These communities, the Lamans and the Banjaras, are constantly on the move. But there is also a spiritual meaning to this song. As one travels on the road of life, one must take care. The tune is also very sweet.

Another song Murlidhar taught me:

Raajan chaalya chaakri
Dhar kaandhe bandook

Keto saage le chalo
Ke kar salo doo took
Oh ji Umrao, thaari boli laage me to mari jaa.

In this song the singer's husband has set his gun on his shoulder and is off to join the army of the King. His wife tells him to take her with him or turn the gun on her. In other words, she asks him to kill her with a single bullet. On hearing these words, the husband says that her sweetness has slain him.

Another song was:

Mhaara chudlera shingaar ji
Thaane likh likh patiyaan haari
Saas nandan-ne pagaa laagni
Devar ne aashish
Mein chha thaari chhabri
Dola, mhaapar kya ki rees
Aan milo gangora pahila
Deejo mati bishaal ji
Mhaara chudlera shingaar ji

The song describes how Rajasthani women wear bangles that are tight upon the wrist and heavy too. And so a Rajasthani woman who says, in a letter to her husband that she has put on her bangles means that she has gone to a great deal of trouble to dress in her best. She says that she is tired of writing letters to him for he never replies. She asks, 'Am I the one you love? If so, why this anger without reason? I send my salutations to your mother and your sister and brother. May God bless them all with understanding.'

Many years later, I saw *Reshma aur Shera*, a film with Sunil Dutt and Waheeda Rehman. It was set in Rajasthan. The great music director Jaidev had composed a beautiful maand, '*Tu chanda main chandni, tu taruvar, main shakh re*' (You are the moon, I moonlight; you are a tree, I am a branch.) It was sung beautifully by Latabai.

Once Allahjilaibai had a music programme at Tejpal Hall in Mumbai. My son specially took me to listen to her. She was in full form and sang a powerful maand that evening. In reality, she was quite old but her voice was still powerful, still as sharp as a knife; her breath control was perfect. She sang four or five maands with ease, as if she were doing nothing more stressful than rolling cotton wicks. Jaidev was sitting at the back.

Here is one more Marwadi song that I remember:

Woman: *Thane kaajliyo banaaoon*
Mhaara nainaasoo lagaaoon
Raat palkaa maa baandh kar raakhoongi
Man: *Gori paalkaana maa neend kaiyya aaveli*
Woman: *Dola palka paalniyo zhulaaveli*
Thaane motidi banaaloon

Woman: I will turn you into kaajal
And smear you in my eyes
All night I will keep you safe in my eyes
Man: How will you sleep, my beauty?
Woman: I will cradle you in my lashes
I will cradle you as a pearl
In my nose-ring, so you will hang near my lips

There is a Rajasthani play called *Dhola Marwan*. It was extremely famous all over Rajasthan. This song is from that play. It is a beautiful composition. This idea is used in a Hindi film song by Mukesh and Lata. It became very popular. Pandit Indra taught me another Hindi song in those days. It goes like this:

Mera chhota-sa Gopal
Hoga kal Jawaharlal
Thumak thumak galiyan vich dole
Bole bol lubhaaye
Saath-saath Jai Hind pukaare
Vande Maataram gaaye
Meri ho gayi goad nihaal
Mera chhota-sa Gopal.

My young son, Gopal
Will one day become Jawaharlal
He will walk through the streets singing
And win every heart.
He will cry out Jai Hind
He will sing the Vande Mataram
My womb shall be blessed
By my little Gopal.

You can see the patriotism that filled the heart in those days. People like Pandit Nehru and Gandhiji and Sardar Patel earned the love and admiration of the common people. When Pandit Indra put the paper with the words in my hand, I was overcome. Independence was close enough to feel its breath. Much was going on in the nation. Mumbai was also going through some dramatic changes. A new and auspicious chapter was beginning in the life of the nation.

And in mine.

I got married.

*

It so happened that *Magarmachh* had the role of an 'instant poet' which means the kind of man who makes up poems on the spur of the moment, whatever the occasion. We had an actor, about thirty years of age, playing the role. He was dark-skinned and lean of build. His hair was combed back. He had a fine straight nose and lustrous eyes. His name was Jaydeo Mishra. He did not speak much and kept himself to himself. People began to call him Mishra or Mishraji. Someone said he was Pandit Indra's disciple. He was generally to be found talking to Pandit Indra or Pandit Dadhich or Pandit Pacheria. Otherwise, he was quiet. But he was a good actor. Later, I got to know that he had been working in Master Vinayak's Prafulla Pictures where he had written screenplays. Master Vinayak had entrusted him with dialogue and direction too. It was Pandit Indra who had recommended him to Master Vinayak. Mishraji was originally from Allahabad. He was from a well-known family. His father, Balabhadra, had been in the police force and had risen to quite a high post. The British had sent him to Central Provinces and Berar. The head office was at Amravati which meant that Mishraji's early childhood had been spent there. He spoke beautiful Marathi—but, of course, all this information came much later.

Mishraji asked Pandit Indra whether I would marry him.

Panditji asked me, 'Do you like the boy?'

I said, 'Please speak to my mother.'

And so my mother, Pandit Indra, Pandit Dadhich and Pandit Pacheria held a high-level discussion at Pacheria's house. Aai spoke in her usual Konkani Marathi. Mishraji was also there. He acted as translator and did quite a creditable job of it too. Aai asked Pandit Indra, 'Will this Mishraji look after my daughter for the rest of her life?' It was a fair question. At that time, we knew nothing about Mishraji. What we knew about him was to do with his professional life. We knew that he had come to Mumbai to work in the theatre. The Pandits gathered there reassured Aai. 'Sushila is as a daughter to us. We will not let anything bad happen to her. You can rest assured,' Pandit Indra said and so Aai agreed to the marriage.

I married Pandit Jaydeo Mishra on 24 October 1947. It was the festival of Dussehra that day. On this day that celebrates a victorious crossing into home, I crossed some boundaries too. Sushila Lotlikar moulted and out of her emerged Vandana Mishra. I was twenty years old when I got married. There was a reason for this. I was earning very well. I had even acquired some little fame as an actress but Aai was worried about how I would get married. It was difficult to find a suitable boy in our caste. This had come to her attention very soon. She had tried in two or three places and had been refused. The families in question said that as Saraswat Brahmins they did not want a daughter-in-law who had acted on the stage. And then there was my mother's nursing. The mother a nurse and the daughter paints her face and prances about on the stage? They wanted nothing to do with such a family.

In those days, it was difficult to find a match for a girl who was on the stage, in cinema or in theatre. Men's sins were all forgiven. Even today, there is a general feeling that girls from good families should not go into films. When an actress marries it is a still a matter of astonishment. There are a number of instances of actresses who earned fortunes and are very successful but find it difficult to marry. Theatre and cinema bring huge quantities of money, fame and glamour. In this world, men and women indulge in relationships and of course women must bear the brunt of society's self-righteous rage. I do not mean to say that all actresses are models of good behaviour and have high ethical standards but their peccadilloes pale in the face of the behaviour of the male actors. I know of many successful actors, directors and producers who do not hesitate to exploit women and treat them as playthings. It is my good fortune that I did not encounter any of them during my career. I started working in Marathi theatre with Altekar Dada and Mama Warerkar who stood firmly behind me.

I found myself in Gujarati theatre after that. The Shree Deshi Natak Samaj people behaved with dignity. The head of the company Uttamlakshmiben ran everything with an iron hand. She herself was a woman so she took particular care of the female actors. The other senior men were Pandit Indra and Pandit Pacheria who treated me with affection. Still, Aai was worried about my marriage. 'Babi, however much we take care of ourselves the world of cinema and theatre is like a coal shop. Your hands are going to get black. However much care you take, people look down upon this world. And as you get older, it will become more and more difficult for you to settle down. It would be best for you to get married as soon as you can,' she said to me often. She did not insist I find someone from our caste and that is why when Pandit Indra told me about Mishraji's proposal and I asked her to look into the matter, she accepted the proposal.

We were in good economic health then. We had about thirty to thirty-five thousand rupees in the bank. Even though I was earning well, we had not stopped saving money. We had no great desire for expensive things. We lived within our means. Both Kashi and I liked saris and I had a fondness for flowers. Babu was working in Shaw Wallace. Now all the responsibility for the family would be his. 'Babi does not have to bear the burden of the family now,' Aai said. Kashi got married after I did. She married a little late. His name was Samandam Nayagar and he was a gentle, good-natured Tamil businessman of good character. Kashi was now working as a health visitor in the Municipality. She was doing well. I had married a North Indian man and Kashi's husband was Tamilian and so Aai chose a Saraswat girl as a daughter-in-law.

To make up for having doubted him, Aai made a one-tola ring for Mishraji and had a sherwani stitched for him as well. She also bought me a Banarasi sari. I already had jewellery. Aai bought all the vessels and other traditional ceremonial items. My wedding took place in the Sitaram Podar Girls' High School, Fanaswadi, Girgaon. Those were days of rationing. Strict rules had been laid down about what you could or could not serve. And so Mishraji had only twenty to twenty-five family members and close friends over to Mangalwadi for a meal. In the evening, in that very hall, we had the reception. Because of the rationing rules, we could only serve ice-cream. Only

Mishraji and a select number of my friends were present at the ceremony.

Prithviraj Kapoor said, 'Mishra, you have gained a wife but you have murdered an actor.'

For Mishraji and I had decided that after our marriage I would stop acting.

Dinkar Patil also came to the wedding. He had worked in Prafulla Pictures and was Mishraji's friend. Later, we went to their house for lunch.

My mother-in-law came down from Amravati for the marriage. She was a lovely person by the name of Kesarbai Mishra. She was originally from the Oza family of the Baliya village in Uttar Pradesh. When she married Balabhadra Mishra, she came with him to Amravati. My father-in-law died an untimely death. Kesarbai was only twenty-two at the time, with an infant on her hip, but she did not weaken. She knew what would happen to her if she went back to her in-laws and so she decided to stay on in Amravati. My father-in-law had bought some land there. He had also bought an orchard in his son's name. Kesarbai decided to live on what she made off this land. She was also blessed with a very sweet voice. She sang bhajans beautifully and her fame began to spread. She formed a bhajan party of three or four people and began to travel with it. They went as far as Nagpur and Wardha to sing bhajans. The people of the area also looked after her. They called her *buaji*, the equivalent of the Marathi *atya*, which means paternal aunt. Her Marathi had the Vidarbha accent and diction but in the Nagpur and Amravati area there is a distinct North Indian influence. A large number of Hindi speakers live there. These people had a great respect for 'Buaji'. In our country, bhajans are sung at every rite of passage. From birth to death, my mother-in-law had a huge repertoire of Hindi and Braj folk songs. She also had a wonderful sense of humour. On the basis of that, she had survived. When her husband had died, she had not given up hope and resigned herself to her fate. She faced what was coming with strength; her life was exemplary. She and my mother were both women of courage. There were hundreds of thousands of women like them at the time and there are even today. They are the rocks on which their families are built.

I must say that my mother-in-law never once expressed any opposition to our marriage. I was, after all, from Maharashtra. My language was different. I was a Saraswat. Mishraji was a Champaranya Brahmin. But my mother-in-law accepted me as a daughter-in-law with great love. She told me all about the Mishra family. She also said, 'We don't believe in caste. We are nomads at heart, pilgrims and seekers. Your husband had many friends from the Teli Tambolis, the Malis and the Muslims. So don't bother too much about caste. Babu (she called her son Babu) is a hot potato; I'm dropping him into your hands. You'll have to take care of him now.' We got married and one week later, Sasubai went back to Amravati.

Mishra tried to get her to stay in Mumbai but she refused to listen to him. 'This is where the two of you will begin your new life together,' she said. 'My life is back in Amravati. I have so many people to see to there. And my trees and the plants will be waiting for me.' She never lived for any extended period of time with us in Mumbai. Her home was in Amravati, Baakdyachi Wadi, which was dear to her. Mumbai was not her home. She could manage about four days before she was ready to return home. But she did come when I was pregnant and stayed for two-and-a-half to three months at all three confinements.

Mishraji was originally from the Karchhana village in Allahabad. It's a village in which everyone's surname is Mishra. My mother-in-law did not return when her husband died. This upset the Mishras. A young widow was obviously in rebellion. What could she be up to? And now her son marries a Marathi woman. This upset them even further. There were no relations between us and the Mishras of Karchhana. Later, in 1964, one of Mishraji's friends, a man named Sharma, went to Allahabad on work and also visited Karchhana. When he told them where he had come from and that he knew Mishraji, he was welcomed warmly. When he had told them all his news, one or two of the elders said to him, 'Tell Babu that he should leave his wife and children and come to Karchhana. We'll find him a wife from our caste. Tell him he can begin again here, start life anew. And if he does not agree, tell him that we will disinherit him. If he writes to us, we will assume he has accepted our offer.'

A week after his return from Allahabad, Sharma came over with the message. Mishraji just laughed. Sharma said, 'There are some magnificent trees on their lands, trees that even ten men would not be able to measure. It is a huge property that your family has. When they cook rice, it is of such high quality that a lovely aroma spreads everywhere. If you wish, you could sue them for your rightful share.' Mishraji laughed again.

When Sharma left he said to me, 'Babi, all of Uttar

Pradesh's homes are riven by dissension over *jad* (jewellery), *joru* (women) and *jameen* (land). We aren't going to fall into that trap.'

Needless to say, he did not send that letter.

I worked on two Marathi plays before I got married. I acted in *Sharda* for a club. I played Sharda. The songs in this play were sweet and lovely. *Ja, ja vaalyacha gheuni ye pankha* (Go fetch me a fan made of khus), *Mhataara ituka ne avghe paaunshe vaymaan* (He's not really so old; only about three-quarters of a century); *Tu shrimantin khari shobhsheel* (You'll look lovely as a rich lady) and especially *Murtimant bheeti ubhi* (Fear stands in front of me). *Sharda* was performed at the Damodar Hall in Parel. In Atre's *Udyacha Sansar*, I played Nayana. Kesarbai Bandodkar played Karuna and Shaili was Shalini Mardolkar. It was directed by Vasant Savkar.

*

Mishraji did not want me to work after marriage. There were reasons for this. In those days, the husband of an actress was viewed with suspicion. It was generally believed that he had married her to live off her money. He was not seen as much more than her manager. Perhaps it will be difficult for people these days to understand the tensions of those days. But an actress's marriage was quite a sensation. I was earning extremely well in those days but I did not want people to talk about us. And so I decided to give up the stage. To tell the truth, I was also a bit bored: those endless shows; and if there were no shows, rehearsals; and all those late nights. I had started working at the age of fifteen. Diwali and Dussehra meant only more shows. There were no holidays for us. I felt the need for a break. Besides, I wanted my own family. I wanted children with a deep yearning. I had begun to feel that the more I worked, the more I'd get trapped in the world of theatre; and that as I grew older, the question of my marriage might end in a full stop. Aai also saw this. 'When both my girls have families of their own, I'll be free of responsibility,' she would say and so I settled down happily to the new role of 'The Wife'.

*

After the wedding, I came to Mangalwadi where Mishraji had a room. It was in Gill Mansion (later renamed Sneha Sadan). Mishraji shared the room with a friend who moved out. Almost as soon as I moved in, I developed a very bad cold. The coughing and sneezing nearly drove me to distraction. The doctor said it was because I had spent most of my life in a mud building and had now moved into a cement one. But then nearly all of Mumbai is a concrete jungle. Is that why the city's residents are so prone to coughs and colds and breathing troubles?

I remember 15 August 1947 very well. The country was independent. Everywhere in Mumbai, an extraordinary excitement, a great wave of enthusiasm washing the city. Everyone was out on the streets. People were hugging each other. 'Mahatma Gandhi ki jai,' resounded in the city. 'Bharat mata ki jai' and 'Vande Mataram' were heard everywhere. People were giving each other sweets. The sweetmeat shops refused to take money. The government buildings were lit up in the night. That day too I had a show somewhere but as I walked to it, I felt a lightness in my step, as if I were floating along. The tricolour was fluttering from every building. Aai had cooked kheer with puris.

India gained independence and in two months, I was locked into the state of matrimony.

Five months later, Gandhiji was assassinated. I was at home. Mishraji was out somewhere. I heard the news on the neighbour's radio. And immediately the *Ram dhun*, *Raghupati Raghava Raja Ram*, began to play. Sadness spread like a dark cloud. Mishraji abandoned whatever it was he was doing and came home. 'Babi, Mahatmaji is no more,' he said in Hindi and sat down on the bed. Our home was on the ground floor. In front was a maidan. There the Rashtriya Swayamsevak Sangh had its shakha meetings every evening. That evening too, the RSS met as if nothing at all had happened and around this time, Kashi came to see us. She threw open the windows and shouted at them. At least today they could call off their meeting. They left quietly.

Gandhiji is still blamed for much these days, especially for his role in Partition. I don't know enough to comment. All I know is that when you say terrible things about Gandhiji, his followers do not burn your home, they do not seek to make your whole life not worth living. This is his legacy which is still alive with us today. Try it with any of the other political leaders and see what happens. Their followers won't let you live.

Here's another thought: The tree that bears the most fruit often has the most stones thrown at it. So it is with Gandhiji.

*

When we got married Mishraji did not have a job. He had left Prafulla Pictures. He and Vinayak had had differences of opinion. 'I have learned a great deal from you but I must now set aside the crutch of Prafulla Pictures,' he said and left. A few months later, in the fateful month of August 1947, Master Vinayak died out of season. Mishraji had a great deal of respect for him and Shantarambapu. He felt that both of them were masters of the techniques of the cinema. V Shantaram excelled in creating the mise-en-scéne while Master Vinayak had an excellent understanding of the mechanics of romantic comedy. Vishram Bedekar was also one of his favourite directors.

After he left Prafulla Pictures, Mishraji was asked to write the songs for the film *Rivaaz*. The stars were Ishwarlal and Paro. Mishraji wrote all the songs—eleven in all. The music was by Rewashankar Marwadi. He was originally from Rajasthan. He played the harmonium beautifully and had a fine understanding of Rajasthani folk music. The film was not very successful but people liked the music. A Calcutta newspaper noted that the music had come out really well.

Here I would like to tell you a story. The world of Hindi film song has been enriched by many Bengali and Punjabi music directors. There can be no doubting their contribution in producing a number of beautiful songs. But few have acknowledged the contribution of Marwadi music makers to the Hindi film song. Khemchand Prakash, Master Ghulam Mohammed, Pandit Jamaal Sen, all came from Rajasthan or the Rajasthan-Gujarat border and enriched Hindi cinema with their beautiful melodious songs. '*Thaade rahiyo, oh baanke yaar re*'

(Stand and wait, my fine dandy) in *Pakeezah* is an excellent example of how a folk song can be adapted to the needs of a Hindi film. From the North of India came S N Tripathi and Chitragupt, two other music directors who have been unjustly ignored. That the sounds of Bengal and Punjab came to dominate the industry happened for understandable reasons. But that is no reason to ignore the other music directors.

K Dutta is another excellent music director who is also ignored.

*

Let me tell you a little about Maangalwadi. I lived there for twenty years. It was like a little village. Three clinics, two grocers, one goldsmith, a laundry, a flour mill, two milk shops, one coal store, a printing press, a greengrocer, a haircutting saloon, a paan shop and a Muslim graveyard. What more could one want?

The wadi was clean. On either side, two- or three-storeyed buildings crowded about. Dwij Vihar, Kumar Vilas, Krishna Nivas, Sneha Sadan were the buildings' names. Our Sneha Sadan was a rather proud building. For one, it was seven storeys high. It even had a lift. There was a small maidan in front of it. Seventy per cent of the residents were Marathis; twenty per cent were Gujarati. There were no Christian or Muslim homes. Christians lived mainly in the Chira Bazaar area or in Khotachi Wadi. We sometimes saw Muslims in the wadi because of the graveyard. There was a mosque behind it. Smack-dab in the middle, a small alley ran through Mangalwadi. This was called Aatli Wadi or 'the inside wadi'. There goldsmiths, banglemakers, tailors and gardeners lived. In front of Sneha Sadan was a chawl. Every Thursday and Saturday, bhajans would be sung there. On Wednesdays, the big draw at Sneha Sadan was the *Binaca Geet Mala*[2].

At Sneha Sadan, most people were well-educated. A doctor, a lawyer, a government collector and a professor were among those who lived in the building, adding their prestige to it. Its main gate opened out into our wadi. There were two wings, A and B, with separate entrances. We lived in the A Wing. Our windows were always open. Many of the residents of B Wing would stop a while and chat to Mishraji before going on. All evening, this would go on. Some people would stand and talk to Mishraji for an hour or forty-five minutes but if they were asked to come in, they would refuse, saying, 'No, no, it's getting quite late already,' but continue chattering away. The A Wing folks would simply walk in for our doors were also always wide open. The children were young and would run in and out of the house as they played. And so we had a board put across the door. One day, one of Mishraji's friends did not see the plank and walked right into it, slamming his knee. He vanished as suddenly as he appeared. Mishraji followed him out, and found him in the wadi, hopping around on one foot as the wadi folk looked on amazed.

'What are you up to?' Mishraji asked.

'That board on your door,' he ground out. 'I don't think I shall ever forget it.'

---

[2]Binaca was a toothpaste brand and its *Geet Mala* (or Garland of Songs) was one of the earliest hit parades of Hindi film music, hosted by the legendary Ameen Sayani on Radio Ceylon.

That poor board! Its name was ruined unjustly.

Tatya Harshe (Shriram Harshe) and Laud Dada (Anandrao Laud) made our days at Sneha Sadan unforgettable. Harshe, Laud and Mishraji were the building's famous triad. Simple affection was the basis of their friendship. There were no expectations attached. We looked upon Tatya Harshe as a saintly man. He was extraordinarily intelligent and peaceable. He was mild-mannered although he held an important post at Sachivalaya. He wore a dhotar and a white shirt. In the evening when he came home, he changed into a shirt and knee-length grey shorts. He was a man of few words. When he contributed his mite to a discussion, he was measured in his language and would express his ideas with clarity. Laud would also turn up. He was an interesting character. No community function at Sneha Sadan was possible without him. He was a good mobiliser and manager of events. Whenever he was surprised by something, he would suck his thumb like a little child.

These three would have far-ranging, free-flowing discussions that could take in religion, society, ethics, politics, theatre and cinema, Acharya Atre's editorials—there was no limit to what could be discussed. When it was time for the Ganapati festival, the conversations became almost incessant. Sometimes, the three of them would go to the Metro to see an English film. When they got home, they would begin a meticulous dissection of the film. When I remember those long discussions, I feel tears coming to my eyes. Those conversations must have had a long-lasting effect on the cultural development of the children of Sneha Sadan. It is a sad comment on our whirlwind world that neighbours no longer find the time to get together and talk about the state of the world. Would it be so impossible for us to slow down? Mishraji would say, 'Babi, the young should have the opportunity to listen to some fine ideas.' In a way, it is part of their education and it may be why we value the oral tradition.

Ganapati was a hugely important festival in Sneha Sadan. Many people took ten days holidays for it. Around July, a flurry of arrangements would begin. When the organisers of the festival got together, it seemed as if a conference of wise scholars were holding high-level deliberations: Appa Deshpande, Aaba Dalvi, Bapu Ranade, Dr Chandratre, Nana Nimkar, Baba Desai were the leaders of the group. They were charged with creating a detailed programme of the festival and Anandrao Laud and the others were in charge of making this happen.

There was always a huge debate over whether Hindi film songs should be allowed at the festival or not. The young wanted the songs, the elders were dead against. Two or three of them were firm in their opposition. One senior resident was positive that he did not want to hear '*Tu hai mera prem devta*' at the festival. He took particular exception to the line, '*Ang lagao pyaas bujhao/Antarghat tak pyaasi hoon main*'. The young simply wanted to listen to *Mera naam Chin-Chin-Choo/Raat-chaandni main aur tu*. At every game of musical chairs, this song was always played. In 1964, Sneha Sadan celebrated the silver jubilee of its Ganapati festival. We put up a play written by Tatya Harshe called *Mangalakshata* (The rice thrown at a wedding). There were no male characters in the play. Mishraji was the director. The women of the building acted in the play. The songs were set to music by Mr Bhole and Kalyani Paranjape acted and sang extremely well. Vimal Samant also did a good job. She was the wife of the well-known animation expert and actor Vasant Samant. Both were extremely warm people and truly hospitable. We became friends during the production of *Mangalakshata* and the relationship lasted for a long time.

Tatya Harshe enjoyed the show a great deal. He was specially delighted by my performance as Sita Kaku. Before the show, the rain came pouring down. Everybody set to work with buckets and brooms and the show went on when the rain went off. It went well. Padmakar Deshpande's wife—they lived on the second floor—wrote a special welcome song for the play and sang it too. The first lines were:

> *Mangalakshata Natak lihile stri paatraanche Harshe yaani.*
> *Tyaat bhoomika saadar kelya Sneha Sadanchya striya-mulini.*
> (The play Mangalakshata was written by Tatya Harshe
> And it was enacted by the women and girls of Sneha Sadan.)

Shashikala Deshpande was very good at public event management. Her voice was also very sweet. For *Mangalakshata*, I went on to the stage after a gap of seventeen years. It felt good. On the occasion of the silver jubilee, the young people of the building also staged a play called *Babhulgaoncha jahagirdar* (The Jahagirdar of Babhulgaon), directed by Nandu Kadwe, fourth floor, A Wing. He also played the lead. He held an important post in the advertising department of the *Indian Express*. Nandu's younger brother, Sharad Kadve, was Raj Kapoor's cinematographer.

In those days, almost every wadi celebrated festivals like Ganpati, Navratri, Republic Day and Independence Day with great enthusiasm and a cultural programme. That meant the local actors and performers were given some recognition. They acquired the status of celebrities in their areas. In our building, Sharad Kantak lived in the B Wing. He sang Mohammed Rafi songs beautifully. It seemed as if Rafi himself were singing. He had a beautiful voice and he found a way to make those Rafi songs his own. He was very popular in Mangalwadi. Padmakar and Shashimami Deshpande's children, Ranjan and Mangala Bhole, were also very good at singing. Bala Jategaonkar drew beautiful pictures. He would use waste material to make beautiful things. These local artists did not care about fame or money. It was enough for them that they were popular in their areas and that they made their friends happy. When Bala Jategaonkar sat down to build a house of Extra-Strong Sweets, all the children would gather around, transfixed by his skill. When Sharad Kantak began to sing *Khoya khoya chaand*, the neighbours would gather to listen and praise him. Once Mangala Bhole sang the ghazal, *Rehte the kabhi jinke dil mein* from the film *Mamta* on the last day of the Ganpati festival and her opening notes were so perfect that even Mishraji set aside his book to stand at the window and listen. Tatya Harshe's son Suhas played the tabla beautifully. These local performers brought pride and energy to the wadi's performances. Another good thing was that one learned how to work together on festival committees. People learned how to mobilize and how to organize. This is why Girgaon has so many cultural organisations.

Sneha Sadan had a Mali Mama. His job was to keep the building clean, release the water from the tank and clean the area too. He was short and chubby. He was very tanned. One eye had a cataract in it. He always wore a khaki bush-shirt and shorts. His wife Anandi, was rather tall and wore a nine-yard sari which reached her knees and a big kumkum on her forehead. Both were outspoken but innocent people. They had their own distinctive way of speaking to each other.

'Oye Anandi, where have you gone to die?' Mali Mama would ask of his wife in an affectionate manner.

Back would come his loving wife's reply: 'I warn you, I will tear your tongue out and slap it into your paw.'

They both lived in a tiny brick-sized room on the ground floor of A Wing. When his work was done, you would find Mali Mama sitting at the main door. When the postman asked where Mishra lived, Mama would snort: 'No Mishra lives here.' He'd drive him away saying in Hindi, '*Abhi tum jaao*.' (Go away now.) The postman would insist: 'Look, this is the address. See? Mishra, Ground floor, Sneha Sadan?' At this Mama would rage at the postman: 'Read-shead. Are you a big barrister? Didn't you hear me telling you no Mishra lives here?' Hearing the kerfuffle, Anandi would come out of the room. 'Hold on a moment. This idiot knows nothing.' Then she would turn on her husband. 'What is it with you? Of course Mishra lives here, right next to us.' And then Mali Mama would say, 'Uhm, that's right. I clean forgot.' Then he would turn on the postman as if it were the latter's fault. 'Don't you get it? What are you doing here? He lives right there. On the right. Come on now, move it.'

Mishraji's name had been mauled into Isram by Mali Mama. He was an expert at this: messing up your surname. He would send people looking for the Kanades to the home of the Ranades. He would take the letters meant for the Shahs to the Patels and if anyone accused him of creating confusion, he would mumble, 'I'm a dunderhead. You know that.'

One day, he had a near-brush with death. It was about five in the morning when he went to check on the water tank. As he climbed on to the tank, he slipped. As he fell, he got hold of a pipe and found himself dangling from it, seven floors above the ground. He managed to get a foothold on a parapet outside Laud's house where he began to try and rouse Laud who was, of course, asleep.

'Arre Laud, are you sleeping? I am dying here. Get up, get up. I am dying and you're snoring, you deaf So-and-So.'

Finally his cries did manage to raise the sleeping Laud and he went out on to his gallery and quickly sized up the situation. He tied bedsheets and clothes together to form a rope and brought Mama back to safety. Mama hugged him in a vise-like grip which he only released when Mrs Laud brought him some hot coffee. 'You came and saved me like a God,' he said, again and again. Then he touched Laud's feet and left.

This was around the time we left Sneha Sadan. That means it was around 1966. There was a government milk booth near the maidan close to our house. In the afternoons, Mali Mama would sit there. One afternoon, the milk van arrived and as he was taking the turn, the driver lost control of the vehicle and hit Mali Mama and landed him in the hospital for a month or two. Gangrene claimed his left foot and it had to be amputated under the knee. After that, Mali Mama was never the same again. All day he would sit at the main door of A Wing and ask, 'Anandi have you seen my left foot anywhere?' From time to time, she would get angry and retort, 'It's gone for a walk. Now shut up and sit there quietly.' This would shut him up for a while.

Around 1963, the Patwardhan family came to Sneha Sadan and instantly became the children's favourites. Vinayakrao Patwardhan was an Income Tax lawyer and his wife Vandana was a well-known teacher in Saint Columba's School in South Mumbai. But we found that out later. When they came to live in Sneha Sadan, they had just got married. A new flat was being readied for them in Tardeo. They lived in Sneha Sadan for only a year but they won over everybody with their civilized and elegant behaviour. Vinayakrao called my youngest girl Gaulan (Milkmaid); Mithila and Ambarish's fights would be taken to him for resolution.

In 2013, Vinayak and Vandana celebrated their golden anniversary. Vandana came over to Borivali especially, with an invitation. She looked as beautiful and dignified as ever.

Dr Vishnu Dutt Arora was a god-send. As a child specialist, he was quite renowned. He had studied in London. He had acquired a great deal of knowledge in the area of paediatrics and was working at the

Bombay Hospital. He had started a clinic for children in Mangalwadi. He had given a great deal of thought to the health of children. He did not believe in simply administering medicines and prescribing ointments. If you took a membership in his clinic, he would take charge of your children's health and give them regular check-ups. He would work out a programme for their health and well-being which included a diet plan and an exercise schedule. He would be concerned about the child's daily routine, its defecatory and urinatory habits, how much it played and how much it ate.

Dr Arora and Mishraji were great friends. He was a short fellow with a round and shiny face. His eyes blazed with his knowledge. I raised all three of my children with his help. He was not above using 'grandmother's remedies'. When Ambarish had mumps, Dr Arora ground up the leaves of the dhotra and told us to apply a poultice of them. He did not prescribe expensive medication without reason. It seemed as if he could make my children feel better simply by laying his hands on them.

Mishraji wrote a play called *Reshmi gaathein* (Silken knots). The main character's name was Vishnu Dutt. This coincidence brought them together and they became friends. In 1966, Dr Arora of the cheerful countenance and happy nature died suddenly. He was not even fifty years old. I still remember him with a great deal of affection and gratitude.

*

Now, a little about my life and my world. I have already told you that Mishraji had written songs for *Rivaaz*. He then worked with Jayant Desai for a while. Desai was a well-known film director of the time. But after a year or so, Mishraji left Desai's unit. At around this time, a South Indian director sent his man to meet Mishraji to ask him if he would like to work in Madras. At that time, many well-known film producers from Madras were planning to make Hindi films.

'Try working with us for the next six months or so. If we work well together, you can bring your family to Madras too,' the director suggested.

But there were many problems with this. I had just given birth to a baby girl. She had been born prematurely at seven months. We named her Kuntala because of her thick curly hair but her pet name was Kunu. (I would also call her Baby which was the habit in those days. My mother called her Kunti and her siblings called her Didi.) We had to feed her with cotton balls soaked in milk. If Mishraji went to Madras the question was—where would I stay? It was not possible for my mother-in-law to leave Amravati to come and stay with us. I could not go to Amravati either because of the extreme weather of the Vidarbha. Dr Arora was not sure that Kuntala would be able to take it. It did not seem possible for me to go back to my mother's house for six months. Our home in Ramji Purushottam Chawl was small and Babu's family was growing. Finally, Mishraji turned down the Madras offer. Other writers from the Hindi film world such as Pundit Mukhram Sharma and Rajendra Krishan made their mark in Madras.

In the middle of all this, Mishraji wrote a Hindi play *Reshmi gaathein*, based on the Moliére play *Sganarell* (*The Imaginary Cuckold*). One could also say that

G B Deval's *Sanshay kallol*[3] (Storm of suspicion) was also based on it; or so Mishraji wrote in his introduction. The Hindi society of Mumbai had organised a festival to mark the hundredth birth anniversary of the pioneering Hindi writer Harishchandra Bhartendu in September 1940. Part of the festival was a show of *Reshmi gaanthein* in the St Xavier's College Hall. The audience loved the play. Saraswatibai Bodas played Lakshmi (the equivalent of *Sanshay kallol*'s Kruttika) while Shalini Mardodkar played Malti (Rcvati). Mishraji directed the play. In 1964, the play was staged again at the Mumbai Marathi Sahitya Sangh in Girgaon. I played Laxmi, Mishraji played Vishnu Dutt (Phalgun Rao) brilliantly. Joseph Dias was Madhav (Ashwin Sheth) and Malti (Revati) was played by Pramila Walawalkar. The show was rather good even if I say so myself.

Then a theatre company began to do shows of *Reshmi gaathein* in Indore. We had no idea about this. The first we heard of it was when the senior actor-director Dattatraya Keluskar told Mishraji about it. Mishraji had a friend in Indore called Surendra Kothari who had a film business. He wrote us a letter to say that the play was doing booming business in Indore. Mishraji had forgotten to insert the notice saying that all rights were reserved or that permission had to be sought from the author when he had published the script. This was what Natya Bharati had taken advantage of. When he heard about it, Mishraji did write to Baba Dike of Natya Bharati. Dike did come

---

[3]*Sanshay kallol* by G B Deval is a play about how suspicion leads to confusion—and a few hearty laughs.

to Mumbai and did meet with Mishraji. They could not agree on the number of shows and later we heard that Natya Bharati had stopped playing *Reshmi gaathein*. Dike was a famous personality and Natya Bharati was a well-known institution. This did not stop them from doing a play without permission. Most theatre companies ignore the playwright's copyright. They're actually experts at this.

In the Natya Bharati version, Vishnu Dutt's role was played by Baba Dike and Suman Dharmadhikari played Lakshmi. In 1969, Sumantai came to Mumbai from Indore. She played the central character in M G Rangnekar's *Aale Devajichya Manaa*. She found her feet in Mumbai's theatre world. I also played a small role in the play. More of that later…

*

Reshmi gaathein was highly praised. Hamid Sayani (Amin Sayani's elder brother and a very fine broadcaster himself), Vijay Kishore Dubey, noted actor Premnath and Pandit Daudutt Upadhyaya were among the theatre aficionados who liked the play. The principal of St Xavier's College liked the play so much that after the show, he went in the middle of the night to Whiteway & Laidlaw, got it opened and bought a Parker pen and presented it to Mishraji. The Hindi theatre of that time was yearning for plays that could relate to contemporary realities. *Reshmi gaathein* filled this lacuna to some extent. Mishraji had carried Moliere's play across the years to give it a new context. The humour was extraordinarily sophisticated.

I thought that Mishraji would now find a niche in Hindi theatre in the city. But that is exactly what did not happen. In cinema, the Bengali and Punjabi filmmakers had already put together their teams. Famous writers like Bhagwati Charan Verma, Amritlal Nagar and Sumitranandan Pant had become tired of the world of cinema and were preparing to go back to Lucknow or Allahabad. They could no longer fit in and did not have the money to set up their own theatre companies. Now what? This question confronted us. We had a toddler on our hands and so Mishraji decided to take a job and do theatre on the side. This was when Jaidev Singhania helped him a great deal. He and Shankarlal Bajaj were Mishraji's closest friends. We had a great deal of respect for them. They helped us through some tough times and were both with us in our happiness. Jaidev Singhania put in a word with Kudilal Sekhsaria. And things got interesting.

Mishraji had a great understanding of astrology but he did not style himself an astrologer. He had decided early that he would not make money out of his knowledge. Vedanta, Shankar Bhashya, Patanjali's yogasutras, Lokayatan Sanskriti, Madhava, Ramanuj, Kanad, Bhakti Sampradaya, Sufi texts were all part of his eclectic and voracious reading. His guru was Hanmant Nevasa Katve. You might find it suprising that someone who was so learned in philosophy and Sanskrit was in Hindi cinema. I found it odd too but so it was.

And so too it was that the wife of the owner of the India United Mills was pregnant. The doctor told her that they would have to operate but he also added that it would be possible only to save the life of the mother or the child. Singhania told Mishraji to check the woman's horoscope. At first, Mishraji was unwilling. Finally after much hesitation, he asked for the woman's horoscope. When he had examined it, he had good news. Both the woman and the child would be well. And so indeed it turned out to be. The industrialist was delighted. Immediately, he put Mishraji down for a job in India United Mill Number 5. His job was to organize cultural programmes for the workers. Mishraji worked there until 1972. His writing came to an abrupt halt. During this period, he only wrote a single one-act play called *Titli*. A few shows did happen. Was this also in Mishraji's kundali, I wonder?

Mishraji never cast his own horoscope, nor mine, nor the children's. He would only sit down with a horoscope if a friend insisted. This might happen once or twice a year but his predictions were always accurate. He seemed to have an internal voice to guide him. In times of distress, he did not seek the advice of the stars. We never asked him nor did he tell us. We did go through some trying times but he would say, 'This too shall pass. We must stand firm.' I do not remember him ever performing a pooja for something for himself. He did not believe in fasting or penance. He did not ask God for anything. On the other hand, I performed pooja every day. He did not stop me either. He said that one should not make a display of one's faith.

I do not remember Mishraji telling the children stories about Rama and Krishna. But as they grew up, he told them incidents and stories that would illuminate various aspects of Indian history and culture. When friends came over, they would talk about the epics, Gautam Buddha, Charvaka, Shankaracharya and Islam. Mishraji had made a careful study of Islam. He spoke Urdu beautifully. Mirza

Ghalib, Mir Taqi Mir, Dr Iqbal, Firdaus, Amir Khusrau, Premchand and Rabindranath Tagore were his idols. Before our marriage, he had spent a couple of years at Santi Niketan. This was when Tagore was still alive. Acharya Hazari Prasad Dwivedi of Shantiniketan advised him to read Kabir. After that Meera, Ras Khan and Surdas followed. Culture, religion and history were his favourite subjects.

Whether it was because his father died young or because he was the only child of his mother, Mishraji was a loner. Respectable society might find him a bit rustic. He never sat cross-legged on the floor for a meal. He would squat when he sat down to eat. He was quick to anger and was terrible when in a rage. We would all cower in fright. When his friends had gathered and there was an argument, you never knew when he would reach ignition point. He expected the house to be kept in good order. If things were not in their place, it would really disturb him. But his temper was also quick to cool. He loved his children a great deal. When he had occasion to scold them or to administer a salutary slap on the back, he would make up with a box of sweets. He did not offer the children excessive love. He tried to make them responsible citizens.

I had three children. Kuntala was followed by Mithila after two years and Ambarish came after another two. The children did not give us much trouble. They were terrified of their father but he was also their friend. Mithila and Ambarish inherited their father's talent for writing. Kuntala became an excellent homemaker. She was a good cook and enjoyed feeding people. She was the fairy of the house.

One night, a thief came to the Inside Gully of Mangalwadi. When he was discovered, the entire area resounded to cries of 'Thief, thief'. All of Sneha Sadan was roused. The excitement lasted for two or three hours. Finally, he was apprehended and everyone went back to sleep. Kuntala was about three or four years old then. I told her, 'They've got the thief. We can put out the lights and go back to sleep.' Kuntala was a little worried. 'They've caught him? Well, shouldn't they be shouting, 'Caught the thief, caught the thief'?' she asked. Mishraji and I had a good laugh over this.

As a child Mithila was plump and fair. She looked European. When I took her to the temple or the market, strangers would come up and praise her. One day, Mithila decided to stick some matchsticks up her nostrils. I was in the kitchen. She had been playing by herself in the corner. Just when I thought it was all right to leave her alone she came up to me and said, 'Ma, look what I have done.' My heart stopped beating for a moment. Dr Arora did not have a clinic in Mangalwadi that morning. So I called him at Bombay Hospital. 'First, get the sonar to pull out the matchsticks. If there's any bleeding, call me and I'll come,' he said. There was a goldsmith called Vaidya in the wadi. He was a nice man. He took out the matchsticks, one by one, using a pair of small pliers. Mithila soon grew impatient. 'First give me some pedas and then you can touch my nose,' she demanded. It was only after I bought her two hundred grams of pedas from Sandu's shop that she allowed us to continue.

Speaking of pedas reminds me of the time when I was pregnant with Ambarish. Mishraji had got two kilos of pedas. I began to eat pedas all day. Every other moment, I had my hand in the box. This was pure irresponsibility on my part. Ambarish was born a blue baby. Dr Arora was furious. Does anyone eat so many pedas? A whole host of doctors took turns to watch over Ambarish, each taking a shift of three or four hours. Finally, he got better but he was always delicate. All three children gave their parents much joy. None of them behaved badly without reason or gave us an opportunity to feel shame over something they had done. When Mishraji got angry, they would all three fold their hands and say, 'Please forgive us, please forgive us'. Mithila was a bit cheeky. She would say, 'Go, we have forgiven you,' mimicking Mishraji's voice and he would laugh, restored to good humour. He loved his children to distraction. When they fell ill he would take it to heart, even though it is in the nature of young children to fall ill. 'Only when things fall to the ground do they rise up again,' my mother-in-law would say. Mishraji did not understand this. He would sit by the bedside of the child, bring gifts of dried plums. The child would get better but the demand for plums would not abate.

*

In 1964, I directed a one-act play for Mumbai's Shrimati Nathibai Damodar Thackersey University. Rehearsals were from three in the afternoon. Kuntala was about fifteen or sixteen years old. School ended around twelve thirty or one o'clock. I would bring her home and then go for rehearsals. During that one month, the responsibility of the house fell on her shoulders. She managed it splendidly. She did everything for her two younger siblings. Mithila was averse to housework. If you asked her to clean rice, she would say, 'Anything but that.' But she was very intelligent. Both Mithila and Ambarish were quick to learn things. When Mithila was in the eighth standard, she learned many lovely poems in Marathi and Hindi by heart. Ambarish followed her in this. She was good at studies. Even as children, both Mithila and Ambarish were bright and could memorize things quickly. It would take them just one reading to memorize something. Mishraji was particularly attentive to them learning things by heart.

Ambarish was in a convent school. He always stood first. He got prizes in all the subjects, except mathematics. The prizes were generally in the form of books. They were all beautifully printed with attractive pictures inside. They were all in English, fairy tales and lovely stories. They seemed more valuable to us than jewellery. Mishraji had a wide circle of friends. Every evening, our small house at Sneha Sadan would be full of people. Discussions too would take place on a wide range of subjects including literature, arts, theatre, cinema, politics and sociology. Mishraji also played the harmonium very well. We had a harmonium and tablas at home. Mishraji knew many traditional compositions, chhands, dohe and ghazals by heart. He had a great love of classical music. Kuntala and Ambarish studied music at Deodhar Master's school. Mithila learned kathak. Mishraji would go to the classes with the children. I do not remember him ever asking them about their schoolwork but he was always willing to expand on the finer points of *Raag Yaman* or he would explain the beauty of a paran (a percussion piece) in kathak. Those were halcyon days and even to think of them can bring tears to my eyes. I can hear the sound of Mishraji playing the harmonium and I see vivid pictures of those days.

Mishraji did not believe that the world ran on the power of money. He had no sense of economic good behaviour. When money came in, he would be happy and he would spend it on us and on close friends with lavish generosity. He might have a coat stitched for himself and then give it away to a friend. He took no thought for the future. He had a big collection of shoes. This is at the time when he was doing well. There were loads of boots, chappals, pumps and mojris. One of Mishraji's friends came over to the house and spotted a brand new pair of pumps. 'Arre, Babu, that's a great pair of pumps,' he said meaningfully. Then he stooped and put on the shoes.

Mishraji said, 'They suit you. Take them.' There were many instances of this. I would get angry when people took advantage of his generosity. My anger would show on my face. Mishraji did not like this. From time to time, we would have rows over this. I would point out that these so-called friends had never so much as invited us over for a cup of tea. Mishraji did not understand this. 'We've set up house. People are going to come and visit. We cannot be backward in our hospitality. We must give of whatever we have and we must give it with love. We cannot discriminate,' he would say. And what could I say to that? The world, in turn, found Mishraji an eccentric. Every year, Navratri would be celebrated at the Mahalaxmi temple with a jatra. Mishraji would take me and the children to the temple but he would not set foot inside. He would remain outside while we went in and made our offerings.

'The children should see the festival,' he would say. 'That's why I brought them here.' Then he would add: 'But the priests and pandas are always caught up in the service of the rich. Why should we go into such temples?'

At that time, Mishraji's beliefs and his behaviour seemed revolutionary to middle-class bourgeois society. He did not have the children ritually shaved even though he was a Brahmin. He had tablas and a harmonium at home. His wife had been an actress. Conversations in the evening would often be about theatre and the performing arts. People were not very sure about us.

The children and I thought of Mishraji as a gandharva who had had a curse put upon him. While he was involved in the world of cinema and theatre, he had none of the vices common to these callings. He did not drink nor did he play cards nor frequent the races. He did not womanize either. He did not use a hookah or a chillum but he never gave up smoking.

While at the Shree Deshi Natak Samaj, I had taken up smoking too, just for fun. I don't know whether my family knew or not. But before we got married, Mishraji told me, 'You'll have to give up smoking.' I did but he never did. From time to time, I would get angry with him but then I would imitate Mithila imitating him and say, 'Go, we forgive you your offences.'

Mishraji died of cancer on 30 January 1982. He was sixty-four years old. A man of integrity, a seeker of knowledge, a maverick, left the world and it was no wiser. The ten years before that had been tough going. Mishraji never complained. He would take out the harmonium and sing Saigal songs or a thumri by Siddheshwari. But things got so bad once that we had to sell the harmonium. Mishraji was as one bereaved; for two or three days, he wandered around the house, lost. The children and I felt very sorry for him; we wanted to weep. All of us fell to work. Mithila finished her matric and took up a job immediately. Ambarish would finish his homework and would make greeting cards which he sold from door to door. We had all made up our minds that Mishraji should not want. In our own ways, we tried to make that happen. Our sons-in-law—Subhash Jadhav and Mithila married in 1975 and were divorced in 1996—also respected him.

I had not married Mishraji in the expectation that he would get rich and famous through the cinema. I wanted a cultured, gentle man as a husband. That is what I got. The children got a good father. In 1966, we had left Girgaon and come to live in Borivali. The children grew up in North Mumbai. Mishraji's South Mumbai friends were left behind and so Mishraji made his children his friends. He did not have money but he offered them a philosophy of life. He nurtured their hopes and dreams. He used to have long conversations with his children. Even if the harmonium had been sold, we still had our music. Nor did the dream of a better tomorrow ever grow dim. He would always see the best side of human nature wherever he could.

All this in the Borivali house.

Here, where I'm writing my memoir.

On Stage Again

We left Sneha Sadan because the children were growing up and the space was now too small for us. In that period, many Marathi families were moving from Girgaon and Dadar to larger homes in Thane and Kalyan, Dombivali or Borivali and Dahisar.

Our departure saddened Anandrao Laud and Tatya Harshe as well as the other neighbours or so they said when they came to meet us. All our friends insisted, 'You must find somewhere close by,' but that proved impossible. When the truck filled with our belongings left Mangalwadi, my eyes filled with tears. I was a Girgaonkar, through and through. I grew up there. I began to work there. I began my married life there. Girgaon had given me my culture. It had taught me valuable lessons in living. That one should help one another; that one should live in harmony with everyone; that the search for knowledge was important and learning was important; that humanism should be nurtured at all costs; that the arts and literature must be respected. This is why people from Girgaon are strong and simple.

But that is not to say that young boys and girls did not go about together. They did flirt and they did have a good time but it was all very circumspect out of respect for their elders. Fear of the family, of the neighbours and their teachers kept them in line. All the girls studied well. They got good educations and some even went abroad to study. Some married outside caste and community too. Inititally parents objected but eventually things would go back to normal. When something untoward happened in our building there was always an army of young men at hand. Virag and Vilas Laud, Ramesh Kantak, Papa and Nitin Nadkarni, Mohan and Suhas Harshe, Nandu and Suhas Ranade, Ranjan and Ashok Deshpande, Appa Naik, Nandu Gavaskar, Kishore Dalvi, Shashi and Arun Mali. The modern notion of privacy had not spread very far in society. People tried to live together and also tried to keep from interfering in each other's lives.

I had lived in Mangalwadi for nearly twenty years. What do I remember of that time? Women used khaki-coloured face powder and Afghan Snow cream. They did up their hair with flowers and gajras. Some women wore the five-yard sari, mostly handloom or nylon. Girls wore frocks and when they turned thirteen or fourteen, they wore skirts and blouses. The skirt always reached beneath the knees. Very few women used lipstick. On occasions such as weddings, a necklace of pearls was a mark of being from an aristocratic family. Men wore shirts and trousers. Older men—dhotars and shirts. When they came home from work, the fatherlog changed into banians and lungis. The women called the banian 'the ganjifrock'.

At various places, there were paan shops. Many homes had the betelnut habit. We too had a brass dabba at home. The popular cigarette brands were Capstan, Panama and Piwla Hathi (Yellow Elephant). You could buy loose cigarettes at the paan shop. It was not the habit to carry full packets of cigarettes in one's pocket or to take them home.

People loved the radio. '*Kaamgar Sabha*' (Workers' World), '*Vanita Mandal*' (Woman's Hour), '*Aapli Aavad*' (Your Choice) were the popular programmes. At a later stage, it was 'Punha Prapanch' (The Family Again) that everyone listened to. Hindi cinema was of course everywhere. Hindi film songs were loved by all. C Ramachandra, Naushad, S D Burman, O P Nayyar were the music directors of note. Shankar-Jaikishen produced hit after hit, as if a string of firecrackers were going off: *Junglee*, *Asli Naqli*, *Jab Pyar Kisise Hota Hai*, *Dil Apna Aur Preet Parai*, *Saanj Aur Savera* and *Gumnaam*.

Mishraji's favourite song was *Bahaaron phool barsao, mera mehboob aaya hai* sung by Mohammed Rafi, from the film *Sooraj*. Various television channels still play songs from that era and I enjoy them immensely.

Raj Kapoor's films were always grand and made with expensive sets. I did not think much of Raj Kapoor as an actor but he was a great director. People would wait impatiently for the films of Raj Kapoor, Mehboob and Shantaram. The young generation would worship Dev Anand. After 1960, Shammi Kapoor challenged his supremacy. My favourite actor was Dilip Kumar. He could make a stone weep with his command over craft. No one has ever come close to that.

I did not get many opportunities to go to the cinema with Mishraji. In the first two or three years of our marriage, we must not have seen more than two or three films. Mishraji would go and see films with his friends. I would see them with Kashi. Later when the children were old enough, we would go with them to see films together. I made it a point to take the children for films including *Goonj uthi shehnai*, *Dharamputra*, *Jhanak jhanak paayal baje*, *Kaagaz ke phool* and the like.

*

In that period of time, one did not know much about divorce nor did one hear of cases of rape. One or two cases might be reported each year in the newspapers. In the afternoons, when a few women got together, they might talk about these things in hushed voices. Their conversations would be replete with disgust, and they always made sure that no young children were around.

At that time only four or five women in Sneha Sadan were graduates. Only two or three of them had jobs. The rest had not studied very much. Most of them had come up to their final year at school or less; but they knew what was important in life. They paid careful attention to their children, their homes and their culture. These were the most important things in their lives. This is what I learned from the women of the respectable middle class.

In the afternoons, the women read the newspapers and magazines. Most houses would get books from the circulating libraries. Magazines too would be borrowed including *Vangmayshobha*, *Hans*, *Mohini*, *Kirloskar*, *Lalna*. They might discuss the important issues of the day. I remember clearly that the women of Mangalwadi were fearfully chuffed when Indira Gandhi became Prime Minister.

We had a neighbour called Kantilal Shah who lived in B Wing. Their windows were exactly opposite ours.

Kantilal's wife, Hemuben, and I were close friends. She wasn't very well-educated. Such schooling as she had had was in a village in Gujarat. She knew no English. Yet, she handled all the bank matters. She had their accounts at the tips of her fingers. She also drove a car. She would pop her children into her Ambassador and drive all the way to Baroda. In those days, we saw Ambassadors, Buicks, Morrises and Baby Austins on the road. Hemuben knew all about these cars and their capabilities. She cooked twice a day and fetched her children from school. And she would take her mother-in-law to the Jain derasar every day.

It would not be proper to apply the standards of today to the women of sixty years ago. Today women have made great strides in every sphere of human activity. There are discussions over women's rights and there has been a general awakening in these matters. This was not so in our time. We had only one way of living—which was to be as peaceable, as understanding and as conciliatory as possible. We were supposed to accept what life gave us uncomplainingly and try to find a way out of our problems. We were not supposed to tell our problems to the world. We were not supposed to share our sufferings with others. We tried to believe that our days of woe were numbered and that days of weal were just around the corner. And so we bore everything and tried to smile.

We hoped that we would find satisfaction at the end of our lives. As Tukaram sang in the film of the same name, '*Avghachi sansaar sukhacha karina*' (I will live happily regardless). There is optimism in this and a beautiful determination, too—and that was life.

*

I felt bad about leaving Girgaon. It meant nothing to the children; they were happy to look out of the windows of the taxi. Mishraji was also quiet. He only said, 'Don't get trapped by a place. Where one lives, where one works, where one builds a good life, that is where home is and that is where one's world is and where one should bring up one's children.'

Mishraji was originally from Allahabad. He spent his childhood in Amravati. He spent the rest of his life in Mumbai. His lifestyle, his food habits and everything else was North Indian. Even his way of looking at the world was North Indian. He said he inherited all this at birth. Yet he accepted Marathi culture with no difficulty. He often said that he was lucky to have come to Maharashtra. He loved Maharashtra, Marathi and the Marathi lifestyle. Even though he lived in Mumbai, he did not seem to miss Allahabad. But I suspect he could have lived in any state or district of India without difficulty. He loved the entire country equally.

*

In comparison to Girgaon, Borivali was a village. When I say this, I am speaking about how it was forty or forty-five years ago. Borivali was then green with trees. At some places, the trees were so thick that the noon-day sun did not reach the ground. There were any number of wells, nallas, canals, groves and small paths. Cars were few and far between. Autorickshaws came later. When we arrived in Borivali we got around by horse carriage.

Borivali was also full of villages with names like Babhai, Gorai, Vajira and Shimpoli. The Gorai Creek marked the far end of the suburb. Somvanshiya Kshatriya and Chaukalshi-Pachkalshi were among the Marathi communities who lived in the villages. There were also Gujarati areas. As the 1960s came to an end, many Marathi families began to leave Dadar and Parel and began to move into Borivali and Thane. Many new houses and buildings began to come up in Borivali.

Our new home was quite large. It was a four-storey building, very long. There were thirteen blocks on each floor and a common passage. There was a toilet and a bathroom in every house. So at one level, each was an independent flat and on another level, it was a chawl and operated like a chawl. It has a long passage as chawls do. From seven a.m. to eleven p.m., the house doors are open. The children run from one house to another, with no fear. Bhagya Nagar was full of Gujaratis. They were all in the cloth or iron markets or they worked in other people's shops. Around eleven in the morning, all the men took the train to South Mumbai. They would all be wearing pyjamas and white sadras. If the sadra had golden buttons, you could tell that the owner was rich. Each one of them would be carrying a briefcase. The people of Borivali saw Mumbai as another city. 'Today, *he* went to Mumbai in the morning,' a Marathi woman from Babhai or Vajira might say. A Gujarati woman might likewise say, '*Tamaara bhai* Bombay *gaya chhe*.' (Your brother has gone to Bombay.) I found this quite amusing. If there was a festival or a wedding, people would go to Mumbai to shop. Things have changed in the last few years. Borivali now has its share of famous shops and shopping malls. In no time at all, Borivali has become Bombay.

In Borivali we saw nature at its best. During the spring month of Baisakh, the sky, the ground, the trees and everything was all burning hot. In the afternoons, the world came to a standstill. Nothing moved, as in the children's game of 'Statue'. Our building stood like a solitary sentry manning a lonely outpost. The open space around us meant that we got a lot of breeze and sunlight.

From our gallery we could see the green hill of [Sanjay Gandhi] National Park. At dawn, the hill was covered with a pink sheen. And then the sun would rise. Mishraji would rouse the children to greet the rising sun. The cold morning air would wake us all up. Each evening, we would see a flock of parakeets making their way home. In the quiet and beautiful areas of the Immaculate Conception Colony, one could even see peacocks. After ten o'clock, no one left the house. Everything became quiet. People slept early. In the middle of the night, the rumble of a goods train might disturb the night. When I heard the whistle of a train on its way to Gujarat, I would feel a strange sensation in my heart.

We all seemed to be on a journey. Stations would pass and fall behind and we would all move on. Our job was to think about the future, not to look back constantly. I loved the song from *Aap ki kasam*: '*Zindagi ke safar mein guzar jaate hai jo makaam, woh phir nahin aate*.' (In the journey of life, the stages we pass will never return.) This is truly what life is about. But it is also true that sometimes stations that we think we have passed suddenly return in different forms. This is what happened to me. I thought I had left the station marked 'Theatre' in 1947 but after twenty-two years, I found myself at the same platform again. In 1969, I began to work as a salaried actress in M G Rangnekar's Natyaniketan. The children had grown up. Mishraji's salary sufficed but I thought I could help a little by earning some money. Mishraji agreed.

Rangnekar was in the process of re-establishing Natyaniketan. He had a brand new play, *Aale Devajichya manaa* (It occurred to God one day) and rehearsals had begun. He had written and directed it. He said, 'Mishrabai, most of the roles have been fixed. I'll give you a small role this time. Do that and I'll put you on as a salaried actor. I'll give you a good role in the next play.' I signed the contract and said to myself, 'One hundred and fifty rupees is not a bad salary.'

Aale Devajichya manaa was a different kind of play. The central character, Vidya Pandit, is a woman of some years who has spent her life working in the cause of women's education. When the play begins, she is about to retire from her job as the principal of a girls' school and marry the man she loves. Her lover, who is an important man in the army, had been waiting for her; he has not married either. Vidya Pandit is dreaming of her new life while her colleagues are delighted at her good news. When we hear that her beloved has been killed in an accident, she is shocked. Then she slowly goes to her table, sits down, wipes her glasses with her sari pallu, and starts to work again. That is the end of the play.

Suman Dharmadhikari did a splendid job of Vidya Pandit but the play did not do well. Still, Rangnekar insisted on doing some shows. Bhakti Barve made her first appearance in a small role as a smart school girl. She had only two or three scenes but she did such a good job that she tucked the entire play into her pocket and walked off with it. At that time, she was working in Akashvani. Everyone in the cast called me Joshibai because that was my name in the play. For many years, Bhakti too addressed me as Joshibai.

Aale Devajichya manaa was a big loss for Natya Niketan. In order to offset this, Rangnekar decided to stage *Bhattala dili osri* (Give the Brahmin an inch and he'll take a mile.). It was one of the great successes of the company. Finding a place to live is always going to be difficult and since this is the theme of the play, it was always relevant. Looking for a place to live, three men and three women rent space in the same house. The result is an interesting play with a fine exposition of human nature. Rangnekar chose good actors rather than well-known ones and directed it well. In Pune, a reputed critic is said to have fallen into a faint, overcome by laughter. Mandakini Bhadbhade played the role of the wife of the owner of the house. She was extremely good at it. Mandakini Tai was a stout woman. Her features were expressive and her body was amazingly flexible. She had a great flair for comedy. When something was happening on stage, she would keep her face expressionless but in such a manner that people found her hilarious. We got on very well. She called me Baayo. Reema was very young then.[1]

'Bha Di O', as it was known, had many shows in the following years. Rangnekar stopped paying salaries and shifted to a per-show system. The rate was fixed at forty

[1]Noted stage and film actor Reema Lagoo is Mandakini Bhadbhade's daughter.

rupees a night. This turned out to be beneficial to all of us. Five shows a month meant two hundred rupees. That was not a bad salary in those days.

*

It will be difficult to find a Marathi person who does not know Khotachiwadi, Girgaon. The Anant Ashram restaurant there is a pilgrimage spot for all those who love fish. Anant Ashram was Khotachi Wadi's jewel. In today's commercialised and speed-ridden world, the residents of the area have not abandoned their relaxed lifestyle. Marathis and Christians live together in harmony in elegant Portuguese style houses. One often feels, when strolling there, that one has stumbled into a Goan village.

At the entrance to Khotachiwadi is a three-storeyed building. Natya Niketan had its offices and its rehearsal hall on the first floor. Opposite the rehearsal hall were two homes. In one resided Krishnarao Chonkar. His daughter Nalini had become famous as an actress. The other home belonged to Gopal Krishna Bhobhe. He sang beautifully and was a renowned musician and critic. He was originally from Goa. He died young. *Dhanya Te Gaayni Kala* (Blessed be Music) was a play he had written before he died. He had gone to offer his play at the feet of the deity of Shree Mangeshi. He placed the play at the feet of the God of Theatre and Performing Arts and breathed his last. It was a beautiful death. His wife was Rangnekar's niece and she lived there with her daughter. Rangnekar directed a production of *Dhanya Te Gaayni Kala*.

Our rehearsals would start at six or six-thirty in the evening. Most of the actors were otherwise employed.

Everyone had a day job and would come to rehearsal from the office.

After cups of tea, we would begin. Rangnekar would sit on a wooden chair and direct from there. It would take about ten to twelve days for us to get our lines by heart. Rangnekar would begin to sort out the business and the moves of the characters once that was done. From time to time, he would make sarcastic remarks in his own signature style. The atmosphere at rehearsals was very calm.

Rangnekar would wear a shirt, coat and a dhotar tucked in and a black topi on his head. His nature was mischievous, his speech pointed and sharp. He would wear wire-framed spectacles, a ring with the nav graha stones and a small pearl-like flower in his button-hole. He walked down the road at a fine clop. He lived in the Grant Road area in a fine building called Model House. He loved little children. The children who acted in Natya Niketan called him Gagga. So did my children. Many years later when my son began to work with *The Times of India*, Rangnekar would joke with him, 'Hey Ambya, the English they use in the *Times* goes over my head. Tell them to send over a dictionary with the paper, why don't you?'

After *Bhattala dili osri*, Natya Niketan did *Sangeet Kulvadhu*. The music was by Master Krushnarao Phulambrikar. When Jyotsnabai Bhole had acted in it, her song '*Bola amrut bola*' (Speak sweetly), based on Raag Bhairavi was a hit all over Maharashtra. She was a beautiful actress and a very good singer. Master Avinash played opposite her as the hero. Jyotsnabai's daughter, Vandana Bhole (Khandekar) was now playing Bhanumati.

Shreekant Pargaonkar of Pune was the hero. I played Parvati. Rangnekar said to me, 'Mishrabai, if you look at it superficially, Parvati is only Bhanumati's servant. But the two of them have a unique relationship. Although Bhanumati is a well-known and populat actor, she treats Parvati as a confidante. She has an affection for Parvati. Parvati, of course, is proud of her successful mistress and she loves her too. You have to keep this delicate relationship in mind when you act.'

Vandana was an excellent Bhanumati. Her voice was beautiful and her songs were popular with audiences. Shreekant Pargaonkar threw himself into his role. Even his songs were inspired. '*Katoo bhavna, daavoo kaisi/Maj dharta janoo karpaashi*' (How do I display the bitterness in my heart? /It seems to hold me in a tight embrace) was one of my favourites. *Kulvadhu* was a hit and so Natya Niketan began doing well. Four or five years later, Vandana played Revati in *Sanshay Kallol*. '*Bholi khuli gavasati ji dhanik vaik bole*' (To catch a rich and innocent young man is our trade) and '*Sanshay ka mani ala*' (Why has doubt entered your heart?) were songs at which she excelled.

I played Megha, one of the daasis of Kruttika. It was a small role, what Bhakti Barve would call a cut-piece role. Raghuveer Nevrekar was magnificent as Phalgun Rao. He had stage presence with a powerful voice and clear pronunciation. Older theatre aficionados were reminded of Ganpatrao Bodas in the same role. The famous singer Ajit Kadkade looked good as Ashwin Sheth and did a fine job of the songs. The scene in the jalsha (the music room) in which Revati organizes a concert was made special by Shobha Gurtu's exquisite and melancholy thumris. Rang

Rupali, Nevrekar's Theatre Company, produced many shows of *Sanshay Kallol.* We rehearsed at Seth Lalchand Hirachand's home. He and his wife were both extremely fond of Sangeet Natak. Lalitadevi was called Bai. She also took great care of us and offered us the best hospitality. After *Kulvadhu*, Rangnekar closed down Natya Niketan. It was a bad time for Sangeet Natak. After the Second World War, Marathi theatre had been affected by cinema. The credit for its revival should go to Natya Niketan.

Rangnekar was originally a journalist. He had a way of using small and intriguing items from the newspaper and exploring them for their dramatic potential. His dialogue was crisp and crackling and witty. His tunes were simple and sweet. This may explain why his plays have lasted for twenty to twenty-five years. In his last days, Rangnekar wrote *He aamche tirth roop* (This, my father). He had even begun work on the production. This was a woman-oriented play and the lead role was to be played by Shanta Jog. By some mischance, Shantabai Jog had a terrible accident. Rangnekar came to me and asked me to play the role and gave me the script. I was even measured for a wig. The advertisements for the play had been printed. But then the actor who was playing the hero suddenly left the play and the curtain fell on the project. After that Rangnekar produced *Pikli paane* (Autumn Leaves). I don't remember whether it was presented under the banner of Natya Niketan or someone else. He wrote for other producers as well. *Pikli paane* dealt with the problems of senior citizens in Rangnekar's traditional subtle and comic style. Mama Pendse was brilliant in the play. Rangnekar cast Mishraji in a large role. The play was not a great success.

Rangnekar then produced a play *Ashram harini* (The ashram deer) by Ashokji Paranjpe. The producer was a man whose name we had never heard. He had absolutely no connection with theatre. Rangnekar gave me a role in the play. N Datta wrote the music, a series of lovely songs. He was a talented music director who has also been unjustly ignored.

Rangnekar put me in charge of the costume trunks. I accepted because it meant a little more money. The play was based on the Pauranic tale of Shakuntala and Dushyanta. Each show ended in a chaotic mess of clothes: shoulder cloths, bark garments, blouses, dhotars, pots, hairpieces, crowns, upper garments. The first production went on rather long. By the time the backstage guests had left, it was quite late. I was afraid that the last local train would leave and so I stuffed the clothes into the trunks and ran.

At the time of the second show, Rangnekar said to me, 'Mishrabai, last time you left in a hurry. I took out all the clothes, folded them properly and put them back into the trunks. Don't do that again. I have agreed to pay you some more to handle the costumes. The last local leaves at one a.m. You will get there on time.' I could have died of shame. After that, I would make sure I put away all the costumes neatly folded when the show was over, from the crowns to the wooden padukas and only then would I leave. It would take about half an hour and often my son would help.

Swayamvar, *Sabhya gruhastha ho!* (Gentleman) and *Kaalay tasmaya namaha* (Salutations to time) were all plays in which I had small roles. *Sabhya gruhashta ho!*

was directed by Damu Kenkre. Since he knew set design well, he made the maximum use of chawl's banisters in the play. Damba, as we called him, was an interesting fellow. He did not say much. He was a master of the business of farce. *Sabhya Gruhastha Ho!* was Jaywant Dalvi's first play. It was an extraordinary comedy. Damu Kenkre, Mandakini Bhadbhade, Ramakant Deshpande, Avinash Masurekar, Vitthal Pandurkar, Ajay Wadawkar, Vachna and Lata Juker constituted the experienced cast. Damu and Lalita Kenkre helped us in a myriad small ways when we were in difficulties and for that I thank them with a deep sense of gratitude.

*

Mishraji died in January 1982 and all my children said, 'Aai, it's time to stop working.' The home front had improved considerably. My son was working and drawing a good salary. And so I made my final curtain call.

I have narrated many memories to you. Time to deal with the present. That done, this book will be done.

I still live in Borivali. I am fast approaching my ninetieth year. I have the usual health problems but I ignore them. My nature is still strong and resolute. Now it's just me and my son at home. Laxman comes in the morning. He washes the clothes and dishes, cleans the house and does other odd jobs. He does not say much but he is good-natured.

My son takes care of me and the house. He cooks well. His kheer, basundi and rawa-besan laddoos are superb. He is a journalist and sometimes writes in Marathi too. *The Times* has allowed him to work from home for which

I am grateful. You could say that Aakash, who lives next door, grew up in our home. Now he is in the final year of a commerce degree. He helps around the house quite a bit. But all our neighbours are nice people.

I get up at six am. I wash my face and offer worship to the sun. When I have got my morning ablutions out of the way, I perform pooja. In the last few years, I have started to read the *Times of India.* I read the words in large type in a loud voice. At one time, Mishraji was very keen that I should improve my English. He got me the *Tarkhadkar Bhashantar Paathmala* (Tarkhadkar Translation Text). Now, in the evening of my life, I'd like to prove to be one of Master Tarkhadkar's ideal students. I'll do as much as I can.

My failing eyesight means I read much less. If I get hold of a really good book, I read it. Five or six pages a day is enough. I'm hardly sitting for an MA, am I? But one thing I will say. Besides education, all is folly. However difficult one's circumstances, one should try to finish one's education. My great regret is that I was unable to study.

Today there is much attention paid to a girl child's education. It was not so in my childhood. If a girl studied, well and good. If not, she could always be married off and then it would be her husband's responsibility. It is a good thing that we do not think this way any more. Today there are many options and opportunities awaiting boys and girls.

But one thing should be kept in mind. The best education gives one a great deal of worldly pleasures. One becomes aware of the state of the country, the time and the circumstances. But to get a feel for life it is not necessary only to get degrees. One should be wise to understand life. For that you need some native intelligence, some commonsense. This is to be found in our very soil in the form of songs, proverbs, moral stories, folk tales, phrases and the like.

Money and power often go to one's head. And knowledge can also be bad for the ego. It is entirely possible to be unjust to others on the basis of one's knowledge. You can also justify your own bad behaviour. So a dry and intellectual approach is not much use to the development of a human being. All of life's problems cannot be solved by the brain and logic alone; if one understands this, it will suffice.

Educated people seem willing to break off relationships easily. They ignore the past and do not think of the future. The working class and the less educated find ways to hold on to each other and to go on living. Has education made us intolerant? Our intellects are stronger, our skills are greater, we have more money now and yet life has become dry. No one takes emotions into account. I have seen this happen in many well-educated homes. I have the feeling this is caused by our education system. Everyone seems to suspect that the other will take advantage of one's goodness. This means that everyone lives in a state of suspicion. Of course, one must bear in mind that we do not always encounter people with kind natures. There are evil and selfish people in the world, even among our relations. I have met my fair share. When they need you, they arrive dripping tears and when they have extracted what they need, they vanish, never bothering to make so much as a phone call afterwards to ask after your health. And yet one must not allow them to poison one's own goodness. That gives them the victory. One must try to retain one's humanity and use it thoughtfully. One might have occasion to help the ingrate but one need not get caught up in such associations. One should expect nothing from such people. And if such a person is in trouble, one should help, but only once. Not again and again. And while one does this, one's mind should be detached and unaffected.

This wisdom has dawned rather late but I remember reading a line in the paper that was attributed to the Gandhian, Acharya Vinoba Bhave. He said that we should try to forget people who stir up evil inside us and expect nothing from them. And slowly I have been able to free myself from the net of old hurts and sour memories.

I note down useful thoughts and quotations I find in the monthly magazines. A good thought can energize the mind. I write a diary. I note the insignificant details of my life. Oh, even things like, 'I drank tea at eight a.m.' or 'Lunch was at one-fifteen'. If a Chinese traveller should come to Borivali, four hundred years from now and happen upon my diary, he would be utterly disappointed. 'An old woman, unemployed, sat and filled the pages of her diary,' he might write in his diary.

Well, let him.

One should not worry one's head about what will happen after one's passing. '*Aprés moi, le déluge*,' as that French king wrote. This line should be marked clearly in one's diary. I do a lot of sewing and embroidery. I make cushion covers. I do what I can. It helps pass the time.

Some neighbour helps me with the threading of the needle. We now have a harmonium again. When we feel like it, my son and I pull it out and sing. My son has a fine and expressive voice. There is no happiness so great as that of singing.

I believe in God. I worship often. I light the lamps in the evening for God before the lights are put on. I believe that no leaf stirs without Him willing it. But I don't overdo it. The persistent worshipper can irritate God. Excessive love is not good for the Gods. From time to time, He should be given a little firing. 'Look, I'm here and I can take care of you,' one should say and set Him straight. But one should offer God one's love too. One should ask for nothing except His blessings. One should not bargain with God.

What good I have accomplished, I ascribe to God. The mistakes are my own. There are people who put everything down to fate and give themselves a free pass. I know an intelligent writer who claims her successes as her own but ascribes her difficult circumstances to her fate. But one thing is true. Whether you believe in God or not, whether you believe in fate or not, you must make your own way. You must work. Tenacity, hard work, innovation, these are what make human beings great. I cannot find it in myself to fast excessively or promise sixteen Mondays or pray and chant. Those who want to do these things, should. But one true mark of good culture is not to worry another with one's observances. Do not make false promises. Do not hurt dumb animals. Do not destroy nature. These are the marks of good upbringing.

To tell the truth, I have begun to worship Nature a little more than God in the past few years. Nature always seems to be at work. Nature knows no rest. The sun, the moon, the stars, the earth, the winds, the rivers, the trees are always at work. They pour their wealth into our hands without making differences. I offer my worship each day to the sun, the moon and the sky. We have a tree right in front of us. I offer a namaskaar to it each morning, without fail.

I end my simple story here. As I take my leave of you I feel a little strange. I have accepted, without complaint, my lot in life. I lived as I thought it best. You will no doubt form your own opinion. Try not to judge me too harshly. One of the sayings I have written in my diary is: Justice should be tempered with mercy. Try to bear that in mind.

I met many wonderful people. I salute all of them. But I salute the few evil ones too. The mind is a wonderful thing, no? I don't remember too much of the difficult times. It seems that only the stories, the people and the anecdotes that brought me joy have remained.

I turn to the authors I have loved—Bahinabai Chaudhury and Laxmibai Tilak—and offer my salutations. And since I have played on the shoulders of the two giants of the Marathi language—Sant Dnyaneshwar and Sant Tukaram Maharaj—it is fitting to thank them with my love.

Author's Note

I am happy that *I, The Salt Doll*, the English translation of my Marathi memoirs, is ready to meet readers. My sincere thanks to Rajhans Prakashan for publishing *Mee Mithaachi Baahuli*, my first literary attempt at age 88, in 2014.

Jerry Pinto's English translation is flawless. He has done a marvellous job and has captured the mood of the Marathi book with rare sensitivity. May Jerry live a long and happy life. I owe this young friend of mine a plate of 'besan laddoos'.

My deepest thanks to Ravi Singh and Speaking Tiger Books for accepting the English translation for publication. Ravi, Paromita Mohanchandra and the entire Speaking Tiger team deserve rich praise for working painstakingly on the English version.

Last but not the least, special thanks to my son Ambarish without whom *Mee Mithaachi Baahuli* wouldn't have been possible.

I sincerely hope *I, the Salt Doll* will win the affection of readers as did the Marathi version.

Vandana Mishra
February 2016

Translator's Afterword

If you have reached this far, you will know already what drew me to Vandana Mishra's memoir. One only has to live long enough in a big city to witness great events: the great Bombay Docks explosion, the coming of Independence, the change from a productive to a speculative economy, the shift in tone and shape of the urban discourse. For me, *I, the Salt Doll* was a book to treasure because of its tone. There is no doubt in my mind that Vandana Mishra is a writer. She has a great sense of timing, she understands the telling detail, she knows when she has to play the fluffy old lady and she knows when to deploy the big guns.

Her story takes in so much of what the city, and so much of what is still the city. Her father was taken from her by a chest infection. This was in the age before antibiotics. (It was only in 1928 that Alexander Fleming first discovered penicillin.) Thrown back on herself, Sushila's mother became a midwife and the family was doing well enough when she suffered an acid attack. Whoever her attacker was, he spared her face but took her career. (That this still happens today should be a matter of national shame. Help stop acid attacks. Go to stopacidattacks.org.)

This forced the young Sushila on to the stage where she morphed effortlessly from a Konkani girl who spoke with a characteristic drawl to an accomplished Gujarati actor, a side heroine; and then a Marwadi actor who wore the jewellery of the rich community on stage as she 'died for love'.

All this before she was twenty-one.

The latter part of her story should have collapsed into

the humdrum routine of marriage and family but it does not. Vandana Mishra has that rare ability: she can, by a trick of tone, draw you into the charmed circle of her family and make you feel at home there. Now you can watch as men bark their knees on boards and babies stuff their noses with matchsticks.

But now that I have read the book several times, I know why I wanted to translate it. I wanted to go back to a time when the city I live in was inclusive and welcoming, a city of workers, where man and woman toiled alike to build the mayanagri of India's imagination. Mishra reminds us rightly of the time before it became a city of the rich, before it prided itself on being the nation's commercial capital and its contribution of the lion's share of income tax. It was simply a city where you could bring your skill, your ability, and you could make a living. It did not matter to that city what language you spoke as long as you made yourself understood. It did not matter to that city what religion you followed, as long as you made yourself useful. It did not matter to that city what you ate or what you thought or where you came from. You were now part of the great kaleidoscope of the city.

I am not among those who believe that this is a culture of the past. I believe Mumbai is capable of reinventing itself again and again. I believe also that we need sometimes to be reminded of who we were to fully aspire to who we wish to become.

Hence, *I, the Salt Doll*.

JERRY PINTO

Mumbai/Bambai/Momoi/Bombay 2016

Translator's Acknowledgements

It takes a village to get a book translated and so I'd like to thank my village.

Vandana Mishra for trusting me with her book. Her son, Ambarish Mishra for offering words of advice and encouragement and for reading the final draft through twice.

Neela Bhagwat for teaching me Marathi formally, again, after a lapse of many years and for listening to my first draft.

Shanta Gokhale, for introducing me to the book, and for listening to my second draft.

Ravi Singh for the assurance of his presence in my life in words.

Andrea Pinto, my sister, for bearing with me when the translatorial fit is upon me.

